Terra Incognita

Terra Incognita

A History of Ignorance in the Eighteenth and Nineteenth Centuries

Alain Corbin

Translated by Susan Pickford

polity

Originally published in French as *Terra Incognita: Une histoire de l'ignorance. XVIIIe–XIXe siècle* © Editions Albin Michel – Paris 2020

Polity Press
65 Bridge Street
Cambridge CB2 1UR, UK

Polity Press
101 Station Landing
Suite 300
Medford, MA 02155, USA

ISBN-13: 978-1-5095-4625-1 – hardback
ISBN-13: 978-1-5095-4626-8 – paperback

A catalogue record for this book is available from the British Library.

Library of Congress Cataloging-in-Publication Data

Names: Corbin, Alain, author. | Pickford, Susan, translator.
Title: Terra incognita : a history of ignorance in the 18th and 19th centuries / Alain Corbin ; translated by Susan Pickford.
Other titles: Terra incognita. English
Description: Cambridge ; Medford : Polity Press, [2021] | "Originally published in French as Terra Incognita: Une histoire de l'ignorance. XVIIIe-XIXe siècle (c) Editions Albin Michel - Paris 2020." | Includes bibliographical references and index. | Summary: "A leading historian opens up a new terrain for understanding the past: the history of ignorance"-- Provided by publisher.
Identifiers: LCCN 2020055368 (print) | LCCN 2020055369 (ebook) | ISBN 9781509546251 (hardback) | ISBN 9781509546268 (paperback) | ISBN 9781509546275 (epub) | ISBN 9781509548033 (pdf)
Subjects: LCSH: Science--Social aspects--History--18th century. | Science--Social aspects--History--19th century. | Ignorance (Theory of knowledge)--Social aspects.
Classification: LCC Q175.46 .C6713 2021 (print) | LCC Q175.46 (ebook) | DDC 303.48/309033--dc23
LC record available at https://lccn.loc.gov/2020055368
LC ebook record available at https://lccn.loc.gov/2020055369

Typeset in 11 on 13 pt Sabon by Servis Filmsetting Ltd, Stockport, Cheshire
Printed and bound in Great Britain by TJ Books Ltd, Padstow, Cornwall

For further information on Polity, visit our website: politybooks.com

Contents

Acknowledgements

My thanks to Fabrice d'Almeida for helping me produce the book; Sylvie Le Dantec, who worked on the text; and Anouchka Vasak, who read the manuscript with an expert eye.

Ah, what hundreds of volumes we might fill with what we don't know!

Jules Verne, *Autour de la Lune* [*Round the Moon*], 1869

A Comprehensive History Implies the Study of Ignorance

The first duty of all historians is to identify lacunae and to inventory and measure gaps in the knowledge of earlier generations and, by the same token, discrepancies in the social reach of what facts *were* known. We cannot fully understand our forebears without some idea of what they did not know, either because no one knew it, or because they in particular were not in a position to know it. This method can be applied to a wide range of fields: think, for instance, of anatomical knowledge, diseases and treatments. It would be an impossibly vast undertaking to write a fully comprehensive history of everything humans have not known and to approach the field in overall terms. To map out what our ancestors did not know, the historian must focus on a single field of endeavour and probe its blind spots and lacunae.

This book focuses on our planet, exploring its mysteries past and present, and the intensity and eventual decline of the modes of terror and wonder it aroused. This means interpreting the history of science and discoveries by studying how the gaps in our ancestors' knowledge were filled, and consequently how the imaginaries and dreams they sparked faded away.

In studying discrepancies in the social reach of knowledge, it is important to draw a clear distinction between various types of scientific unknowns. Some things could only be dreamed of, not explored, such as the seabed and the polar ice caps. Others were observable but inexplicable, such as earthquakes, volcanoes and dry fogs. Yet others were resolved by forms of exploration that slowly restricted the boundaries of ignorance, such as the rise of mountaineering and expeditions to the unmapped hearts of certain continents.

To make my point perfectly clear, let me turn to Jean Baechler. He has argued that in small prehistoric communities, everyone knew the same things. In the village where I grew up, set in the rolling Normandy countryside, most of the country folk who gathered in the local cafés after Sunday mass could easily join in conversation, since they all knew more or less the same things: livestock farming, traditional crafts, what they had learned at primary school and, in the case of the older men, their wartime experiences. Apart from the priest, the doctor, the primary school teacher, the vet and the notary, they all had the same gaps in their knowledge – and even then, an electrician and car mechanic had recently set up shop, further stratifying the local knowledge base to a small extent.

When we read Balzac, Goethe, Dickens and Stendhal, we have to make an effort to understand and imagine the way they thought about our planet, which they saw as a mysterious place, all the more frightening for being beyond comprehension. The depictions of the earth they would have been familiar with were fundamentally shaped by the vestiges of past cultural beliefs; those with little or no schooling must have found it truly terrifying. From the eighteenth century on, knowledge had become increasingly stratified between those described as 'scholars' – the term 'scientist' had not yet been coined – and the vast majority of the population in the West. In the same vein, the history of the stratification of the thirst for knowledge is a fascinating question: this is what philosophers, following Augustine, called *libido sciendi*. It is what makes Flaubert's *Bouvard et Pécuchet* such a piquant read: the novel ironically foregrounds the depth of ignorance and intense thirst for unattainable knowledge that must have tormented many a mid-nineteenth-century clerk.

Identifying gaps in the knowledge of our forebears means tracking the pace of discoveries and public access to knowledge – in other words, how scientific discoveries about the earth, geology, vulcanology, glaciology, meteorology and oceanography were transmitted down the social scale. It also means studying how the earth was illustrated, the depth of its history and geography, the gradual process of filling in the blanks, and attempts to discover the secrets of the polar regions. It is very difficult to close our own minds to the images of our planet that we carry within us. That is the aim, and the challenge, of this book.

The entire period under study was characterized by the triumph, or at least obstinate survival, of localism and restricted horizons, both literal and metaphorical, contradicting our modern perceptions of the vastness of space. This is particularly clear in the history of the perception of meteorological phenomena, recorded on a small local scale from the sixteenth century and gradually expanding to the discovery of the jet streams in the mid-twentieth century.

As I was writing this history of the developing stratification of ignorance, it came as some surprise to me to realize that such gaps were not always considered as shortcomings liable to mar human happiness. The advances of the Enlightenment and the progressive slaking of the thirst for knowledge, *libido sciendi*, had their fair share of detractors, just as the Enlightenment had its own dark side. Take, for instance, Jacques-Henri Bernardin de Saint-Pierre's shrewd essay in praise of ignorance in his 1784 *Études de la nature* [*Studies of Nature*]. He argued that ignorance stimulated the imagination and filled the world with wonders: 'Thanks to my ignorance, I can indulge the instinct of my soul.' On his solitary rambles, he claimed to enjoy the countryside more when he had no knowledge of the chatelains who owed their reputations in large part to their châteaux: 'The ignorance of the scenery is of greater advantage to me than an acquaintance with it. I have no occasion to know that a forest belongs to the abbey, or that duchy, in order to think it majestic. Its aged trees, its deep glades, its silent solitudes, are enough for me.' Contrary to the beliefs of the apostles of the Enlightenment, 'Night gives us a much higher idea of infinity than all the brilliancy of day.'[1]

Secondly, Bernardin de Saint-Pierre, inspired by the natural theology that is a constant feature of this book, wrote that ignorance encourages our trust in God: 'Thanks to my ignorance, I can indulge the instinct of my soul'; 'For one pleasure which science confers and destroys in conferring, ignorance bestows on us a thousand, which are much more agreeable.' It also soothes our fears: 'How many evils ignorance conceals from us.' Paradoxically, it is 'the inexhaustible source of our pleasures'.[2] The same inclination towards the obscure and unknown is shared by several Romantic literary travellers, guided more in their appreciation of the world by the authors of classical Antiquity than by what contemporary science might have been able to teach them.

Researching ignorance inevitably throws up a

number of difficulties. The first is our modern depictions of a planet that we consider our home. The degree of responsibility we feel towards it was barely beginning to emerge in the nineteenth century. The increasing number of threats to the planet in the Anthropocene era are now understood to be a human, rather than divine, apocalypse. This process, which distances us from the understandings of the eighteenth and nineteenth centuries, has progressed at a much faster pace since the mid-twentieth century. It is likely that in times past, no single individual could ever accumulate so much knowledge in the span of their lifetime. I personally feel this very strongly, though I am no scientific expert, and I call on my contemporaries as witnesses.

On Monday, 1 July 1946, I was a boarder at a Catholic middle school in the small Normandy town of Flers-de-l'Orne. The headmaster, a priest, seemed very elderly to me. He had a degree in philosophy, and had in fact, I later found out, studied under Émile Durkheim in the early years of the century. That day, he came into our classroom and told us that classes were to be suspended that afternoon: we were to go to chapel to pray for the earth (*sic*), because the Americans were going to drop an atomic bomb more powerful than the ones that had destroyed Hiroshima and Nagasaki. People everywhere were asking whether this horrifying experiment would not annihilate or lay waste to the earth. We lined up, walked to the chapel and began to pray. No disaster ensued.

The reason why I am sharing this anecdote is because it is significant. The headmaster had, quite unwittingly, swept us into the Anthropocene era by teaching us that man was a terrible threat to what we call our planet.

In my mind, however, it was not as simple as that. We were not allowed to talk at the school refectory.

While we ate, one of the older pupils would read aloud from a book, and I would always listen attentively. I remember being particularly struck by three readings in the course of the years 1946 to 1948. The first was René Caillié's narrative of his travels from 1824 to 1828 to Timbuktu, in the dark heart of Africa, full of slaves but not cannibals. The second, which obsessed me for a while, was about the notebooks found on Captain Scott's body after he tragically perished on his way back from his failed attempt to be the first man to reach the South Pole. Two years later, the older boys read aloud Jules Verne's *Île mystérieuse* [*Mysterious Island*] – and by then I was one of the older boys myself. In short, while the headmaster was ushering us into the Anthropocene era, the books read to us to furnish our imaginations dated from a time when the earth was much more mysterious and frightening, and very different from the earth we were learning about in the immediate aftermath of the Second World War. In my case, the chasm widened yet further as I eagerly devoured many more of Jules Verne's novels.

I sometimes wonder about how I pictured the earth myself before 1957, before the beginning of aerospace history, which has filled our television screens with images of our entire planet seen from on high and from every angle. I find it amazing today that it was not until I was gone thirty that I heard talk of plate tectonics, explaining how earthquakes happened.

Core samples extracted from the polar ice caps are now shedding astonishing new light on our knowledge of the earth's past, while nanotechnologies are teaching us much about the temporal depth of the humans that inhabit it. In a word, the way we picture the earth, or rather the planet, is undergoing a radical upheaval, in a way that goes much further than the constant refrain of climate change and the short-term threats of the Anthropocene era.

These inklings hint at the usefulness of a history of ignorance and an inventory of gaps in the knowledge of each period of history, to give a clearer picture of the humans who lived through them.

Part I

GAPS IN ENLIGHTENMENT KNOWLEDGE OF THE EARTH

1

The Great Lisbon Earthquake of 1755

Pinpointing and understanding the significance of the Great Lisbon Earthquake means looking back at a broad outline of how such major natural disasters impacted the way our ancestors thought, from the medieval period on. On 25 November 1348, Petrarch described watching a destructive tidal wave sweep across the Bay of Naples:[1]

> I had scarcely fallen asleep when not only the windows but the walls themselves, though built on solid stone, were shaken from their very foundations and the night light, which I am accustomed to keep lit while I sleep, went out. We threw off our blankets, and [. . .] the fear of imminent death overcame us. [. . .] The religious of the dwelling in which we were living [. . .] frightened by the unexpected danger, and bearing their crosses and their relics of saints, and invoking the mercy of God in a loud voice, all marched [. . .] into the bedroom I occupied. [. . .] What a downpour! What winds! What lightning! What deep thunder! What frightening tremors! What roaring of the sea! What shrieking of the populace![2]

A century later, Bindo, the Sienese ambassador to Naples, described an earthquake that struck the city on 4 December 1456: 'The great cries, the laments, the great wailing and shouting of men, women and children who ran naked out of their homes in the dead of night, clasping their infants to their necks . . .'. Such terrifying displays of the earth's powers were experienced in a climate of fear, explored some decades ago by Jean Delumeau.[3] Contemporaries read them as interventions by the hand of God, or secondarily as the work of demons. In the cultural background were episodes of Biblical violence, from the Flood (a point we will return to at length) to the destruction of Sodom and Gomorrah and, most importantly, the Apocalypse. Faced with disaster – the term 'catastrophe' was not yet in use – contemporaries influenced by sermons and other religious practices read such events as scourges intended to punish sinners. On a population level, psychological reactions were driven by the urge to save the souls not only of individuals, but of society as a whole. In a world where entering Paradise was the ultimate purpose of life, divine wrath seemed quite logical.

As Thomas Labbé points out, in this perspective, natural chaos was by no means blamed on God; a feeling that the punishment was fair and just and the need for preservation were enough to avoid such a reaction. At that point in time, events were interpreted above all on a local scale, in urban and rural areas alike. Anywhere further afield was barely taken into account, if at all. The materiality of the disaster did not become central to people's concerns until the fifteenth or even early sixteenth century, when disaster culture began to emerge.[4]

Yet there was a gradual change in perspective between the late medieval period in the fifteenth century and 1755, when this book opens. Multiple earthquakes were recorded in this period, with at least twenty-seven causing major damage between 1600 and 1800. Interpretations began to shift early in the period. Disasters were still considered to be God's work, but they were seen less as manifestations of divine wrath – and therefore as punishment – than as signs of His mercy, saving men's souls from damnation. Many prodigious events were interpreted in a similar light.[5]

A further process that helped soften the harshness of divine punishment was that second causes gradually came to be taken into account. This was the belief that God rarely intervened directly in nature, instead letting it work on its own. The seventeenth century saw the development of a reading of divine intervention crucial to understanding the period under study, which I highlighted in a previous work: the physico-theology of Oxford's Protestant scholars, underpinned by the regular Anglican practice of reading the Psalms daily. This school, known on the continent as 'natural theology', studied at length by Henri Brémond,[6] considered the earth as a marvel corresponding to God's plan. It was to be exalted for its beauty, overlooking the brutality it sometimes displayed. This sense of wonderment gave rise to the Providentialism celebrated by the Abbé Pluche and Bernardin de Saint-Pierre.

Prior to the Great Lisbon Earthquake, a series of questions came to change sixteenth- and seventeenth-century images of the Flood, though it remained an accepted historical fact for everyone with the exception of Leonardo da Vinci. Questions gradually arose about how it happened and whether all the consequences associated with it were even possible. Was it one single flood, or were there several? It must be acknowledged that such questions were asked only by an elite few. This was society's solid bedrock of beliefs and questions on 1 November 1755, when Lisbon was struck by a catastrophe (the word was first used in French in its modern sense in Montesquieu's *Lettres persanes* [*Persian Letters*] in 1721).[7] My aim is not to write a history of the earthquake, but it is important to outline it in some detail to shed light on the history of the stratification of ignorance, thrown into sharp focus by the event.[8]

Anne-Marie Mercier-Faivre has argued that from 1755, or roughly mid-century, on, disasters were no longer mere signs, but events in their own right: 'It progressively became a concept that made for a brand-new way of thinking about the world and about mankind.'[9] Stripped of their religious frame of reference, disasters were now open to analysis. Thinking about and trying to understand catastrophes was no longer the sole preserve of the church. That said, a degree of caution was still required. The idea of divine punishment, the fear of everlasting damnation, and the primary goal of salvation had by no means faded from people's minds. Disasters may now have been considered suitable material for analysis, but they were still a reminder of the transience of life, the gift of a merciful God.

On All Saints' Day, 1 November 1755, Lisbon was shaken by four major tremors in nine minutes, starting at twenty to ten in the morning. Clouds of sulphurous vapour darkened the sky. A few moments later, a tidal wave – what we would now call a tsunami – five to six metres in height ploughed across the city, causing devastation in its wake. An aftershock struck at around eleven. Fire ravaged the city for five to six days. Looters caused further panic. The worst-affected areas were the low-lying neighbourhoods in the city centre. It is currently estimated that some ten thousand people died. Few of them were from the city's leading families, who were on their country estates. The king and the royal family were in residence at the Belém Palace.

Though in relative decline at the time, Lisbon was still

at this point Europe's third most important port, after Amsterdam and London. Vast quantities of merchandise were destroyed. Worse, perhaps, in the eyes of the men and women of one of Europe's great Catholic capitals, sixteen churches collapsed, including the patriarchal cathedral. The opera house and thirty-three townhouses belonging to aristocratic families were also destroyed.

We will now focus for a while on how word of the disaster spread. While the tremors themselves were felt across much of Western Europe, it took around a month for the news to reach gazettes and news-sheets. In Germany, a Cologne gazette was first to break the news, on 21 November. The *Gazette de France* [*France Gazette*] printed it the following day. By the end of the month, the news had reached most of the German-language press. Until February 1756, the 'disaster' was often described as a 'dreadful catastrophe', with articles highlighting the scale of the destruction. On 29 November 1755, for instance, a gazette in Bern recorded that 'seven-eighths of the houses in the city of Lisbon were torn down in six or seven minutes'. It informed its readers that three volcanoes had caused a fire and that 100 to 130 locals had found themselves trapped in the ruins. The total destruction of trade in one of Europe's busiest commercial cities was the focus of much interest. News-sheets and almanacs soon followed suit, eager to shed sensational light on the parlous state of the world with many a Biblical reference. Though the term 'catastrophe' was widely used in the press in the aftermath of the Lisbon earthquake, the much-discussed news of the disaster does not seem to have profoundly challenged an optimistic world view and the idea of God's providence, particularly in Germany.

The history of the earthquake involves the event itself, its impact, and the subterranean mechanisms that cause such tremors. Societies of the past – the eighteenth century, in this case – did not know what caused the earthquakes they frequently experienced: as we have seen, between 1600 and 1800, at least twenty-seven quakes caused considerable damage. The 1750s were the second major period of seismic activity since the seventeenth century, even before the Lisbon disaster. Not knowing what caused the tremors was difficult to live with and the disastrous consequences were hard to overcome. Since the numerous sources on earthquakes had no idea what caused them, their principal focus was on the local impact, damage, institutional reaction to the chaos, how the news spread, and on recording the memory of the disaster. The folk memory of earthquakes was also focused on the destruction of urban centres. The many earthquakes that shook France in the seventeenth century were almost completely forgotten, remembered at most locally or regionally. In the latter half of the eighteenth century, however, earthquakes across France were recorded in hundreds of narratives, scholarly and academic debates and dozens of articles in periodicals, maps and catalogues. Scholars began to study the country's seismic activity. The years 1755–64 represent a high point in interest in the topic, before a slight decline. Interestingly, earthquakes became a hot topic for debate prior to the Lisbon disaster, though the event certainly also drove the process subsequently.

From the point of view of a history of ignorance, the most important issue is that scholars began to ask questions: what triggered the disaster and how did it unfold? From 1755 on, the French Academy of Sciences launched a fully fledged earthquake research programme[10] that built an archive of such events. According to the *Journal encyclopédique* [*Encyclopedic Journal*] of 1 May 1756, 'All physicists are working to find the actual cause of earthquakes. [. . .] The cleverest circles [. . .] are making it a topic of conversation.' Of particular interest for this book is the article's claim that 'even the ignorant dare talk about it. [. . .] In a word, everyone wants to discover this terrible secret of nature.'[11]

The mid-eighteenth century saw the rise of subscription libraries and educational and scientific publications. The closing quarter of the century was a golden age of popular scientific debate. In this context, the problem of earthquakes was still widely discussed in fashionable salons at the end of the century. It is no exaggeration to call this the 'earthquake craze',[12] akin to the fashion for hot-air ballooning. Even the rural population took an interest in the topic. The curiosity and suffering caused by the shortfall in scientific knowledge were still intense in the closing years of the eighteenth century, though curiosity about earthquakes was tending to give way to an interest in volcanoes. Even so, a play about the Great Lisbon Earthquake was still being performed in Paris in the very early nineteenth century. As late as 1878, a set of clockwork figures was shown in Orleans, performing two events from history: Joan of Arc delivering the city – and the Lisbon earthquake.

Scholars spent the half-century following the disaster arguing about its causes. Lisbon opened up a space for debate. Three types of explanation were put forward. The first argued for a subterranean inflammation of sulphurous and bituminous matter, attributing the earthquake to an underground fire. The second, which held most sway in the latter half of the century, believed that a dilation in the air triggered the tremors. This explanation was driven by the fashion for studying the physical properties of gases. The third explanation was based on theories of electricity that were highly popular at the end of the century; it held that the disaster was caused by the instantaneous propagation of electric fluid through all conducting bodies.

What is most interesting is that people were now trying to understand the disaster, to interpret it, protect themselves from its effects and measure its impact on society, quite apart from the question of salvation. The catastrophe played a significant role in establishing the earth sciences.

At the same time, a new research focus on fossils and the fledgling study of geological strata led to renewed challenges to the unity and universality of the Great Flood, as scholars began to posit a series of local floods and modify their thinking about the age of the earth.

The Lisbon earthquake and the series of disasters that followed it also had an impact on the emotional range of responses to such cataclysms. From that point on, descriptions of the destruction they wrought and their scientific study went hand in hand with the expression of a feeling of pity and compassion for those affected. There was also sometimes an urge to aestheticize the tragedy – a point I will return to later. A new fear took over from the fear of divine wrath: the potential collapse of civilization. This feeling is still with us today.

We now turn to the cognitive and emotional consequences of the Lisbon earthquake. It was long argued that Voltaire's poem about the disaster set out to radically challenge God's goodness and the optimistic philosophy of Leibniz's *Theodicy*. This is true as far as it goes, but requires further explanation. Unlike d'Holbach, Voltaire did not wholly exclude God from his reflections and his denunciation. He doubtless thought society was not yet ready for a fully secular response to natural disasters. Diderot was more outspoken in his opinion that it was 'the movement inherent in matter, not the will of God that transforms the world';[13]

Jean-Jacques Rousseau held that natural disasters such as volcanic eruptions, major earthquakes and terrible fires caused by lightning were the cause of the social state, since they brought men together in large numbers to repair the damage. More immediately relevant for a history of ignorance are the gaps in knowledge filled by the Lisbon earthquake, which revived *libido sciendi*, the thirst for knowledge. In this context, the disaster proved a turning point. As well as the printed press, handwritten communications in the form of letters and even hand-copied gazettes played a significant role. Later sources documented the importance of oral memory in handing details of the Lisbon earthquake all the way down to the late nineteenth century. Grégory Quenet has argued that the event 'led to an unprecedented unification of Europe, perhaps unrivalled until the French Revolution'.[14] The Lisbon earthquake long remained the archetypal deadly disaster in the European imaginary, almost completely supplanting the Lima earthquake of 1751.

I have chosen to take the Lisbon disaster as a key date marking a turning point in the history of contemporary representations of the earth. Between 1755 and the opening decades of the nineteenth century, a series of questions and issues were hotly debated, demonstrating gaps in contemporary knowledge, the first hesitant steps towards filling them in, and a lack of clarity in how even the most cultivated thinkers pictured the earth and sought to understand its secrets.

It is worth briefly stating the main issues explored as part of this wide-ranging debate, which varied across the social spectrum:

1 How old is the earth? How best to understand the timescales of its history?
2 What is inside the earth? Fire, water or viscous

matter? This question gave rise to theories on earthquakes: when these became fashionable, the same process was extended to volcanoes, with various interpretations put forward to explain the magnificent spectacle.

3 A series of questions focused on the poles, which lay beyond human reach at that point. Did they have inner Arctic and Antarctic seas? Where did sea ice come from?
4 Before the first mountaineering expeditions, how did people think geological strata and mountains were formed?
5 What did they think about glaciers and mountain topography?
6 What was the meaning of the first major fossil discoveries, for instance in Siberia?
7 In an age when men were fascinated by storms and hurricanes, how did such weather phenomena form and grow so violent? (This was a time when remote regions were only just beginning to come into focus, leading to a new interpretation of space – a point I will return to later.)

When studying the history of ignorance, it is crucial to foreground the lack of certainties and the sheer scale of the gaps in common knowledge. Even the most erudite of scholars asking profound questions had barely more information at their fingertips than those content to leave the questions unasked. Since Aristotle's theories had been discredited, undermining the solid core of certainties that had satisfied *libido sciendi* for centuries, Enlightenment scholars were asking many new questions. However, as we will see, very few gaps in knowledge about the earth were actually filled with any certainty. Diderot and d'Alembert's *Encyclopédie*

[*Encyclopedia*] and similar works of Enlightenment scholarship offer the reader an inventory of uncertainties and lacunae waiting to be filled.

2

The Age of the Earth?

Some thirty years ago, I imagined two individuals sitting on the seashore, contemplating the rocks at their feet.[1] One thought he was looking at the remains of Noah's Flood; the other, his contemporary, with some knowledge of the new theories on the age and internal structure of the earth, was studying what he saw as the result of hundreds of millennia of geological history. This imaginary situation demonstrates what I am calling the stratification of ignorance. In this case, the first figure doubtless represents the vast majority of the population – but it is impossible to prove it. What grounds are there for thinking that references to the Flood were still the majority belief and for considering that changes in our understanding of geological time long remained limited in scope? Answering these questions means taking account of the widespread belief in the historical truth of the Flood narrative. It also means realizing that a belief in a long geological timescale clashed with Biblical history, which shaped not just the chronology of the Flood but the broader understanding of all historical time. The sixteenth-century Protestant bishop James Ussher's chronology *Annales Veteris Testamenti* [*Annals of the*

Old Testament] calculated, for instance, that the earth was four millennia old.

Jacques-Bénigne Bossuet's writings are significant in this context. His 1681 *Discours sur l'histoire universelle* [*Discourse on Universal History*], written to educate the French Dauphin, calculates the earth's past based on events recounted in Genesis.[2] It seamlessly connects the early stages of the earth to the birth of history as it was then known, thereby establishing the planet's chronology as Bossuet saw it – from the origins of the earth itself, which he believed he could date, to a straightforward reading of the events recorded in Genesis.

Bossuet noted the date of each event in the margins of his book, from the Creation to Charlemagne's reign. The presence of well-known dates, for instance from the history of the Roman empire, lends an air of legitimacy to the dates of origin that Bossuet makes up with little explanation.

His methodology is interesting: as Georges-Louis Leclerc, Comte de Buffon, was later to do, he divided history up into eras. I will focus on the first of these. It began with the 'grand spectacle' of Creation, which Bossuet's marginal note dates to 'world year 1', or 4004 BC. This meant he dated the Creation to 5,682 years before the *Discours sur l'histoire universelle*. His second date was when earth began to be populated after the Fall of Man, in the year 129 after the Creation. Adam and Eve were in the Garden of Eden for no more than a century or so.

The first major event that was crucial to date was, of course, Noah's Flood. Bossuet pinned it down to the year 1656 after creation, or 2348 BC. After the Flood, he wrote, began 'the decrease of man's life [and] the alteration of diet'[3] which marked the first events of known history. Bossuet's estimation that the earth was six thousand years old, coming from a leading scholar of the last third of the seventeenth century, was widely shared, at least by those who asked themselves such questions. Nonetheless, can it really be argued that his contemporaries did not have the capacity to make the imaginative leap out of Genesis to suggest other time-scales, foreshadowing the coming scientific revolution?

One particularly challenging passage in La Bruyère's 1692 work *Les Caractères* [*Characters*], which I have not found quoted in books on dating the origin of the earth in the seventeenth century, is worth looking at here. La Bruyère, eager to demonstrate the existence of God to free thinkers, writes that God's existence cannot be questioned, even if the date of the Creation were to be pushed back 'Many million years, nay many thousand millions of years' (which he tacitly suggests would be ridiculous). In a word, he continues, 'all Time, is but an instant, compared with the duration of God, who is Eternal: The Extent of the whole Universe is but a Point, an Atom, compared with his Immensity [. . .] what [is] the Extent of that Grain of Sand, which is call'd the Earth?'[4] This demonstrates that at the tail end of the seventeenth century, it was indeed thinkable to picture the earth as billions of years old, as early-twenty-first-century research indicates is the case, even if the idea was then dismissed as absurd.

Diluvial theories, which sought to explain the structure of the earth by reference to Noah's Flood, were around for over a century after the *Discours sur l'histoire universelle*, though without further attempts to calculate the age of the planet. It is worth comparing Bossuet's and Ussher's estimations with that put forward by Buffon a century later: he probably developed it as early as 1749, though it was only published in 1778.[5] Buffon's calculations in *Époques de la nature*

[*The Epochs of Nature*] are not based on Bible readings, but rather on the belief that the planet's internal heat results from a gradual cooling process that began when it was first formed as a ball of fire. Buffon considered his theory to be irrefutable.[6]

Buffon worked on experiments to date the stages of earth's cooling process, which he saw as eras in its history. Arguing that the planet is made up of matter similar to glass, he believed that it would eventually cool to the point of dying, predicting global extinction by cooling rather than the Apocalypse of the New Testament. By his calculations, the earth would become too cold to inhabit in 93,000 years, when humans, flora and fauna, and the earth itself would freeze to death.

According to Buffon, the history of the earth was divided into seven periods. In the first, earth, like the other planets, was a molten mass that took on an ellipsoid shape. It had been known that the earth was flatter at the poles, shaped like a pumpkin rather than an orange, since La Condamine's expedition to Peru in 1735 and Maupertuis's expedition to Lapland in 1736–7.[7] In the second era, Buffon argued, the earth solidified to the core, becoming a great mass of glass-like material that formed the basis of the primitive, non-fossiliferous mountains. He calculated it took 2,905 years for the earth to solidify all the way through and a further 33,911 years for it to become hard enough to touch.

Buffon's third era corresponded to the sedimentary history of the earth once it was solid. The oceans covered the continents and formed calcareous deposits from the shells of sea creatures. The fourth era began when the oceans shrank back and volcanoes developed as slowly accreted combustible matter caught fire. In the fifth, elephants, hippos and other large land animals known to inhabit the hottest regions lived in more northerly climes, where the climate then suited them. In the sixth, the continents split apart and humans came into existence. It then took a further 74,047 years for the planet to cool to its eighteenth-century temperature. Buffon therefore calculated that the earth had formed 110,763 years before. Even then, his manuscripts indicate that he considered the possibility of much longer timescales, up to ten million years.

This matches a clear trend shared by other thinkers, including Immanuel Kant and the early geologists Barthélemy Faujas de Saint-Fond and Jean-Louis Giraud-Soulavie. The imaginary of grand geological timescales that rose to prominence in the decade between 1760 and 1770 is one of the fundamental aspects of the representation of earth's history and morphology. It is impossible to measure how far it extended across the social spectrum, as I suggested at the start of this chapter. Nonetheless, it was the most significant difference in the beliefs of Buffon and his contemporaries and represents the starting point for a decisive stratification between the haves and have-nots of knowledge.

For a measure of this complexity, we now turn to Bernardin de Saint-Pierre's *Études de la nature*, published in 1784, a wide-ranging book that was still shaped by a belief in the impact of the Flood, and more broadly in Providentialism, proclaimed at the same time by Bernard Nieuwentijdt's *Het regt gebruik der werelt beschouwingen, ter overtuiginge van ongodisten en ongelovigen* [translated into English as *The Religious Philosopher, or the Right Use of Contemplating the Works of the Creator*] and Noël-Antoine Pluche's *Spectacle de la nature* [*Spectacle of Nature*]. Bernardin de Saint-Pierre opened with a critique of the hypothesis that the earth was originally molten. He also argued that the sea could not have formed mountain ranges, since it could never have risen to such a level: it had been repeatedly noted since Antiquity that God had set an invisible marker on coastlines that the sea could not pass. In short, the earth's history was entirely shaped by God's word.

Bernardin de Saint-Pierre's views on the poles, tides, currents and sea ice are sometimes strikingly accurate, suggesting his ideas are not to be dismissed out of hand. To the modern reader, they are at odds with his flights of lyricism on the impact of Noah's Flood. Though there is little direct evidence of his influence, Bernardin de Saint-Pierre's renown suggests that many people may have been swayed by his view ascribing 'the general deluge to a total effusion of the polar ices',[8] combined with water falling from the clouds and melting from mountain ice caps. He dismisses the cataracts of the 'great abyss' in favour of a more scientific vision. For Bernardin de Saint-Pierre, the cataclysm was caused by the sun drifting temporarily from its elliptical course, setting the polar regions aflame:

> Then all the plans of Nature were reversed. Islands of floating ice, loaded with white bears, ran aground among the palm-trees of the torrid zone, and the elephants of Africa were tossed amidst the fir-groves of Siberia, where their large bones are still found to this day. [. . .] At the sight of the disorder reigning in the heavens, man, in despair, despaired of the safety of the earth. [. . .] Every thing was swallowed up by the waters: there remained on the earth no trace of glory and felicity of the human race, in those days of vengeance, when Nature involved in one ruin all the monuments of her greatness.[9]

The cascading waters roared into the Atlantic, where they triggered dreadful tides, spreading 'vast beds of shells' and forcing 'counter-tides'. This, he claims, is how expanses of sedimentary deposits came to be formed. The Biblical reference to a flood lasting forty days seems to match the timescale of Bernardin de Saint-Pierre's vision of the polar ice caps melting away entirely. After 150 days, the waters once again froze at the poles and land once more emerged from the waves. Bernardin de Saint-Pierre's Biblical perspective is informed not so much by Genesis as by the Book of Job's 'darksome doors'. In a highly significant passage, he calls on his readers to bear witness as he denounces the ignorance of his contemporaries, challenging them before turning to the Providentialism that was later to undermine his reputation.

What conclusions can be drawn from knowledge, or otherwise, of the earth's age and history at the turn of the nineteenth century? The picture is one of hesitancy and contradiction, with the European scholarly elite split between two opposing visions. This ignorance extended to the earth's history and morphology. In the opening years of the new century, how did Goethe, Jane Austen and Chateaubriand picture the interior of the earth and the planet's history? This question is nigh on impossible to answer, because we have no way of measuring what they did *not* know. What historians must bear in mind is that people were divided between two visions. Before we turn to the mysteries of the polar regions, one of the earth's most widely debated enigmas in the half-century following 1755, we will look not at the earth's history, but at what people believed its internal structure to be.

3
Imagining the Earth's Internal Structure

At this point in history, there was no way of observing the earth's interior directly or drilling for deep core samples. As a result, picturing the insides of the globe meant drawing on preconceived notions or 'understanding(s) of the world based on mythological and literary discourse'.[1] Contemporary thinkers sought to fill this gap in scientific knowledge with a series of 'theories of the earth'. Naturally, they all drew on the theories in Plato's *Phaedo*, which pictured Tartarus, a vast body of water at the centre of the earth, filled by an internal network of rivers of water, fire and mud. This chapter will focus on the most relevant period for this question, beginning in 1650, when theories of the earth began to be published in large numbers, all refuting the Aristotelian belief in an eternal world.

Galileo had begun asking questions about the deep core of the earth, which he imagined to be dense and solid. Theories then began to proliferate between 1650 and 1750, some of them mutually contradictory. Vincent Deparis and Hilaire Legros analyse the writings of Nicolaus Steno, Hooke, Newton, Burnet, Woodward, Whiston and Leibniz, among many others.

Though there is much to be said on these early theorists, their writings are beyond the scope of this chapter, other than to point out that much was being written on the question and to outline the theories that seem to have been taken up the most widely.

The late seventeenth century saw the triumph of Flood geology in the debate on the nature of the earth's internal structure. Thomas Burnet's 1681 work *Telluris theorica sacra* [*Sacred Theory of the Earth*] argued that the Flood had brought about fundamental changes to the globe, reshaping its featureless surface to create reliefs. Burnet explained this massive impact by reference to the 'great deep' of the Bible – a vast internal body of water whipped into a towering storm.

John Woodward's theory, published in 1695, doubtless convinced a wider audience. He drew on the existence of fossils to hypothesize that the Flood had completely dissolved all the matter that made up the earth, then laid down sediment 'in concentric layers in order of gravity'.[2] Woodward adumbrated, or perhaps paved the way for, the Neptunist theories of the late eighteenth century (see below, chapter 5). The following year, Whiston put forward the hypothesis that a comet might have skimmed the earth, triggering the Flood by adding a considerable quantity of water vapour to the planet's atmosphere and causing a crack in the earth's crust, freeing the waters of the 'great deep'.

The theories espoused by so-called 'Flood geologists' were criticized by later thinkers. Henri Gautier claimed in 1721 that the globe was completely hollow and full of air. After an eruption near Santorini in 1707, the vulcanist Antonio-Lazzaro Moro theorized that inside the earth was a ball of liquid fire, while Johann Gottlob Krüger suggested in 1746 that the combined action of the Flood and an earthquake had set the entire world ablaze. The historian Vincent Deparis points out that an impressive range of models of the earth[3] were put forward over the course of the sixty years preceding the Great Lisbon Earthquake. Fertile as the imaginations of these early geologists were in ascribing a major role to Noah's Flood, the well of ideas eventually ran dry; theories on the planet's internal structure took a new direction as research on the issue became less theoretical and imaginative. Kant's 1756 essay 'On the causes of earthquakes on the occasion of the calamity that befell the western countries of Europe towards the end of last year' can be taken as the first step in this new direction.[4] He began by drawing attention to how little his contemporaries knew about the depths of the earth and reminding readers that no man had ever gone deeper than one-six-thousandth part of the distance to the centre of the earth. He then stated that surface phenomena such as earthquakes will one day shed light on the planet's internal structure.

Likewise, Buffon's two books quoted previously discussed the earth's interior, drawing on recent geological discoveries to develop his theory. Following Descartes and Leibniz, particularly the latter's *Theodicy*, he hypothesized that the globe began as a molten mass, seeing it as akin to a cooler version of the sun. Like Kant, he underlined how much he and his contemporaries did *not* know, writing in 1749, 'There are many parts of the surface of the globe with which we are entirely unacquainted, and have but partial ideas of the bottom of the sea, which in many places we have not been able to fathom.' Men had only been able to explore 'the mantle of the earth' since 'the greatest caverns and the deepest mines do not descend above the eight thousandth part of its diameter'.[5]

Buffon did, however, consider that the earth was a

solid, homogeneous globe, not hollow or empty. He theorized that the planet was initially a molten mass that had gradually solidified (see above, chapter 2) and filled with a vitreous material of roughly equal density to sand. He rejected the hypothesis that the core was still on fire. The thinking of later generations was led by geological and physical observations, and the question of the earth's inner structure was set aside for a while. Late-eighteenth-century scholars seemed tacitly to agree that the earth's interior was unknowable, focusing their attention instead on visible phenomena such as geological strata, mountains and volcanoes.

For a period of nearly eighty years, from 1750 to 1830, the main focus of early geologists was developing mineralogy to further their knowledge of the nature of rocks and observing stratigraphy and mineral fossils to identify the successive geological eras that left their mark on the surface of the globe. At this point, it is useful to take a brief look back at a scholar whose work proved far-sighted, though it received little notice in his lifetime. Nicolaus Steno was the founding father of stratigraphy and tectonics and identified the organic origin of fossils, realizing that they were the remains of species now extinct. Decades ahead of his time, he pointed out that strata, or layers of sediment, built up as a result of successive deposits in a liquid environment. He hypothesized that the order of deposits must reflect the order of episodes of global history and that where strata were no longer horizontal, it must mean the earth's crust had moved vertically at some point. Steno founded modern geology a century before other thinkers caught up, but his writings drew little attention and his ideas had little impact on the history of knowledge – and of ignorance.

As shown in chapter 2, one of the two vital issues in filling in the scientific map was the full acceptance of extremely *longue durée* geological timescales in the 1760s and 1770s. The observation of strata now meant that geology became a historical source. This new understanding of the geological past challenged the views of Flood geologists; in the nineteenth century, the argument pitted catastrophists against uniformitarians (see below, chapter 13).

Part I of my book will focus solely on the rise of geology through ever more detailed studies of the earth's surface and visible morphology, collecting evidence for the 'constitution and conditions of the depths'.[6] The debate on representations of the earth in the closing years of the eighteenth century and first half of the nineteenth turned on two main questions. The first was whether tilted strata of sedimentary rocks arose from the way the deposits formed as they were laid down, or whether they bore the traces of fractures from vertical and horizontal tectonic movements, as argued by those who had studied mountain ranges closely. The second, much more heated debate pitted the Neptunists, led by Abraham Gottlob Werner, against the Plutonists, who followed James Hutton. The two scholars studied rocks with a view to 'identifying, differentiating, and giving precise descriptions of the various minerals and rocks that make up the Earth's surface'.[7] Their ambition was to 'describe the visible surface of the Earth as objectively as possible and to identify its principal components'.[8]

Werner's and Hutton's theories – and their followers – were radically opposed. Werner's Neptunism, which dominated the closing quarter of the eighteenth century, posited that water caused sedimentary deposits. All minerals and rocks, including, most polemically, basalt, were initially 'in a dissolved state at the bottom of the primeval ocean'. Werner, somewhat influenced by diluvial theory, argued that the various strata were deposited in turn as they filtered out of the water. At the end of the eighteenth century, Werner still believed that water played a fundamental role in creating the earth. Vincent Deparis rightly points out that the theory did at least encourage detailed examination of the various layers of sediment.

In 1778, however, Déodat de Dolomieu concluded from his study of basaltic lava that it could only come from the interior of the earth as a viscous flow, contradicting Werner's Neptunism. This led to a lively scholarly argument. In 1785, James Hutton joined in the attack on Neptunism, making the case that the earth's inner core was still burning. The heat rising from the subterranean regions was what forced rocks upwards as the cycle of sedimentation continued. This Plutonist theory accounted better than Werner's Neptunism for the very long timescales of the geological past, which many scholars now believed in. Plutonism also had the advantage of accounting for something that was obvious to even the most casual observer: the interior of the earth was still full of fiery matter.

Neptunism dominated scholarly debate until around 1795. Vincent Deparis records a swift change of opinion between 1802 and 1804, at the very end of the period, when studies of the volcanoes of the Auvergne swayed the debate towards Plutonism.

How, then, did early-nineteenth-century Europeans building on Enlightenment science picture the earth, understand its surface and its reliefs and imagine its past? It is difficult to give hard and fast answers, but we can put forward some hypotheses.

It seems likely that most of the population, spending their lives within a very small geographical scope, wasted little or no time worrying about such matters. Their lack of knowledge about far-flung regions – and for most people, even ones closer to home – meant that towns, plains, hills and even the mountains that closed off their horizons were simply features of the earth, as mentioned by the priest in the pulpit preaching from the Book of Genesis. That would certainly have been enough to satisfy the curiosity of those few who did wonder about the past and the shape of the earth, which was to be admired as God's creation. The Flood was generally accepted as historical fact and some might have thought that it was bound to have shaped the planet as they saw it. Almanacs, which were practically the only reading matter available for many people, barely touched on such questions.

Yet the stratification of ignorance was already beginning to grow more complex: amateurs with a passion for science were starting to gather in academies in the provinces, Paris and London, and reading accounts of papers given at scholarly institutions and the books published by their members. They were also able to keep abreast of the latest developments in gazettes. The members of such institutions at the turn of the century were doubtless curious about the history of the earth, what its interior was made of and how it had been shaped. However, it is difficult to measure the extent of this scientific elite and to find out whether artists, writers and political leaders asked the same questions.

Working on the hypothesis that they most likely did, they must have been very confused by the clashing theories, incomplete experiments and inaccurate observations made by the scientists of the day! It is, however, fair to say that unlike half a century previously, most of the elite would now have been relatively comfortable with stepping back from the Biblical narrative and understanding that the earth's morphology reflected a history that was hundreds of millennia old. This was a fundamental stage in overturning earlier representations of the earth.

For early-nineteenth-century thinkers, sedimentary strata and the potential for horizontal and vertical movement, whether driven by water or by fire, and the nature of the fossils entombed in them must have made up a somewhat incoherent data set that would have been difficult to take as the basis for a clear picture of the planet they lived on. It should also be borne in mind that what we now know of glacial reliefs and multiple successive periods of glaciation was at that point wholly unknown, and that mountaineering and mountain exploration were in their infancy. Doubtless the most cultivated travellers – a group we will return to later – were tempted to daydream and celebrate the God of natural theology, gleaning emotional sustenance from the thinkers who codified the Sublime or from the poets and writers of Antiquity. The conflicting, vague, incomplete theories of contemporary science were perhaps less immediately appealing.

Yet there were many other fields in which the map was almost completely blank. We now turn to what was known – and hence what was *not* known – about the polar regions, their seas and the eternal ice that kept them inviolate.

4

The Mystery of the Poles

To understand the long history of ignorance of the polar regions, we need to begin by looking back at the keen interest in the poles in earlier centuries. The urge to discover the North-West, and to a lesser extent the North-East, Passage prompted a number of maritime expeditions hoping to drastically shorten the route to the Indies and the Far East, until eventually the Little Ice Age intensified and made such ventures impossible. The latter half of the sixteenth century saw the first attempts at polar exploration, spurred on by knowledge of the adventures of Erik the Red in the late tenth century and his discovery of a great 'green land' – now simply Greenland – where his descendants lived for several centuries before the line petered out.

Prior to 1600, scholars were convinced that the North-West Passage was out there somewhere. They did, however, stumble on one question: was it possible to navigate the polar seas? Sailors who tried and failed to find the passage claimed it was not, painting dreadful word pictures of the polar region in texts that described 'ropes and pulleys that froze and became stuck', water supplies that had to be chopped up with axes, and impenetrable fogs that left the crew sailing blind.[1] Polar temperatures were described as the most extreme cold found on earth. The sixteenth-century navigator William Barents wrote that the cold 'freezes ears and toes, lips and noses [. . .] and shoe leather and even stops clocks'.[2] The sailors felt 'a blend of terror and stupefaction at the phenomena they encountered even while suffering from them'. Faced with an unimaginable reality, it was hard to find the words to express their experiences for readers. This utterly alien world proved impossible to describe. Their terror was heightened by the threat of dying on an ice-bound ship. Barents's account is dominated by a feeling of sheer repulsion. No aesthetic emotion seemed to soften the terror of a place that every instinct told him to flee.[3] Further expeditions did eventually flesh out some of the cartography of the highest latitudes, though all eventually ended in failure.

The early-seventeenth-century expeditions are more significant for the purposes of this chapter. Henry Hudson found the bay that bears his name in 1600, but his ship became ice-bound. He was forced to hunker down for the winter in appalling conditions; his crew mutinied and drove him off the ship in a small boat, in which he drifted until he died. The British adventurer William Baffin travelled as far as Spitsbergen in 1612–14, reaching 78° north, but was able to go no further. On his return to Britain, he claimed that the North-West Passage simply did not exist. From then on, few expeditions set out in that direction and the polar regions remained an impenetrable mystery for the best part of a century. Willem Barents made several attempts to discover the North-East Passage to the north of Siberia, but he and his men eventually froze or died of scurvy. The beginning of the Little Ice Age and the declining economic significance of the North-West Passage meant that no further attempts were launched until around 1720.

At the same time, exploration of the southern seas began in the 1580s, though with few solid results compared to the richly imaginative picture Europeans had of the region. In this age of maritime expeditions, the poles stirred imaginations to great flights of fancy. Wild claims were made about the polar regions: in 1559, Guillaume Postel wrote that Paradise lay beneath the Arctic. Frédérique Rémy has argued that Europe's shared cultural heritage of myths placed the 'supreme centre of the world'[4] in the far North. In 1596, the famous cartographer Gerardus Mercator drew a map which had the four rivers of Genesis converging on the North Pole, which he depicted as a tall black rock.[5] The British occultist John Dee believed that the earth communicated with the divine realm via the poles. At the other end of the planet, the southern polar region was thought to be a place of wonder, populated by naked men and women who lived by the laws of nature but sadly lacked knowledge of the immortal soul. The same process of myth-making populated the poles with monstrous creatures such as dragons, lionesses and sea-unicorns. The poles were imagined to be sites of strange beings, particularly the southern polar region, which seemed to prompt more richly imaginative tales than the far North. In 1582, Henri-Lancelot de La Popelinière wrote his *Trois mondes* [*Three Worlds*], describing a region filled with marvellous riches and untold delights. More realistically, the Dutch navigator Abel Tasman landed on the island that now bears his name in 1642, describing its inhabitants as small, destitute and naked.[6] A further source of knowledge, which we will return to later, were visible phenomena such as the Northern Lights and the magical polar landscapes. Such data played a part in establishing the scientific importance of the poles, though they still remained beyond reach. As the freezing polar conditions began to extend further south into Europe from 1600 on, long, harsh winters became commonplace. As a result, people began to lose interest in what the poles were really like and turned their curiosity to other objects, such as the Northern Lights, comets, sunspots, the shape of the earth and how flat it was at the poles, and journeys to the centre of the earth.

The seventeenth century, the age of imaginary travels to the sun and the moon, was also the age of polar exploration. In the absence of scientific observations, and therefore reliable knowledge of the poles, Utopias and myths filled the gap. It was sometimes unclear where scientific data ended and imagination took over. Gabriel de Foigny's 1692 *Les Aventures de Jacques Sadeur dans la découverte et le Voyage de la terre australe* [*Adventures of Jacques Sadeur on his Voyage of Discovery to the Southern Lands*] described the inhabitants as hermaphrodites who eschewed sex and food. The *Journal des savants* was convinced it was genuine and categorized it as an actual travel narrative.[7]

The second wave of polar expeditions from 1720 to 1760 – paradoxically, the height of the Little Ice Age – was based on more serious scientific principles. In France, the navy and the Academy of Science began to work together, taking over from the great trading companies. Their aim was to use science to fill in the blanks at the top and bottom of the globe. Astronomers, physicists, mathematicians, doctors and naturalists all took a renewed interest in the poles; many of them signed up for maritime expeditions over a span of four decades.

In 1739, Jean-Baptiste Charles Bouvet de Lozier set out on a voyage to the southern seas, where he discovered the great blocks of ice now known as tabular icebergs. The Danish navigator Vitus Bering set out twice in 1725 to find the North-West Passage, failing in both attempts. He kept trying, only returning home five years later. Travels to Lapland then became fashionable.

After the 1760s, the period that is the main focus of this book, no polar expeditions were launched for forty years. However, scholars remained fascinated by the mysteries of the poles and tried to puzzle them out by the power of thought. The observations made by sailors on the expeditions raised several scientific problems, first and foremost the question of polar ice, in the form of both ice floes and the 'frozen mountains', or icebergs, encountered by the navigators. The old myths took on a new lease of life thanks to the fashion for travel writing and major expeditions led by Bougainville (1766–9), Marion Dufresne (1770–1), Cook (1772–5), Kerguelen de Trémadec (1773–4) and La Pérouse (1785–8). It would be an over-simplification to describe these as polar expeditions per se; rather, they were attempts to fill in the map of the Indian and Pacific oceans.

This generation of navigators set out on a quest to find the *Terra australis*, a continent and trade route offering an alternative to the passages thought to exist in the Arctic region. Though none of the previous voyages had brought back absolute proof of a southern continent, James Cook launched an official expedition in 1772 to locate it. He sailed into the polar circle in January the following year and completed the first circumnavigation of the Antarctic. On his return in 1775, he declared that there was no continent at the south pole, since he had been unable to pass through the wall of ice. As a result, scholars began to doubt the existence of the mythical southern continent and the belief in an idyllic land at the South Pole crumbled along with the hypothesis of the

North-West and North-East Passages, not to be revived for a further century.

This is a vital point for our history of ignorance. For our forebears living on the cusp of the eighteenth and nineteenth centuries, the hopes of new northern and southern continents were crushed. The debate over the North-West Passage and the continent of Antarctica came to a sudden stop. Two long-standing myths collapsed. The dearth of knowledge persisted and perhaps even deepened for the scientists who, for the best part of a century, had physically travelled to the polar regions themselves. For a generation, the poles became at best a conversational topic in fashionable salons, with lively debates on the mysterious nature of sea ice. For centuries, navigators had been describing the terrifying climate on the ice floes that trapped ships, forcing their captains to hunker down for months on end. The debate came to focus on giant, free-floating blocks of ice found in the ocean. Were icebergs chunks of land ice sheared off from the continent, or were they frozen seawater?

It was commonly believed at the time that seawater could not freeze, hence sea ice could not consist of seawater. This was claimed by Buffon, who believed that ice seen in the ocean must have broken away from the continent and been swept along by partially frozen rivers. We now know this belief was unfounded. However, his ideas were widely shared, including by the geographer Philippe Buache, the explorer Pierre-Louis Moreau de Maupertuis and the authors of the *Encyclopédie*. D'Alembert wrote an article on the topic. It was believed that ice could possibly form in bays sheltered from the wind or in the mouths of rivers that diluted the salt content of the seawater. Louis Cotte's 1774 *Traité de météorologie* [*Treatise on Meteorology*] argued that the sea was only frozen along the coast. There was also a belief that there was open sea at the pole itself – a point we will return to later – explained by the presence of the sun during the long northern polar summer. It was thought that the open sea was ringed by ice formed in rivers running along the coast.

In conclusion, expeditions to far northern and southern climes led to what Frédérique Rémy describes as 'spectacular' progress in mapping the polar regions, compared to the sixteenth century. Yet when the great explorer La Pérouse died shortly before the turn of the nineteenth century, the poles remained cloaked in mystery. Arguments in favour of open seas at the pole, the elusiveness of the North-West Passage, the notion that there was no land in Antarctica, and the belief that seawater could not freeze together formed a major scientific blind spot that must be taken into account in attempting to outline the dominant image of the planet at that point in history. At the same time, the partial survival of Flood geology based on the poles, as recorded in Bernardin de Saint-Pierre's *Études de la nature*, fed into and strengthened these erroneous beliefs.

It is incredibly difficult to grasp what was going on in the minds of our forebears, who would have been more or less well read on the discoveries and debates of the day. What mental traces were left by texts full of the imaginary marvels of the polar regions, so popular in the golden age of travel writing? It is hard to tell: for the most cultivated and best-read individuals, they came to overlay Pytheas' Ancient Greek account of his navigation to the far north, the ancient kingdom of Thule and the frozen sea around the poles. Samuel Taylor Coleridge's *Rime of the Ancient Mariner* (1798) sheds some light on the complex interaction of scientific certainties and uncertainties in the minds of men, gleaned from their readings.

5
The Unfathomable Mysteries of the Deep

This chapter brings us to an area of almost complete ignorance for eighteenth-century thinkers: the 'domain of the inconceivable, the incomprehensible [. . .], the unthinkable and unlivable [. . .] the depths of the ocean', as Jean-René Vanney wrote in his magnificent history *Mystère des abysses* [*Mystery of the Ocean Depths*]. He continues, 'The contemporaries of Leibniz [in the seventeenth century] certainly knew no more than the scholastics, who in turn perhaps knew less than Aristotle.'[1] Even a century on from Leibniz, there is a striking lack of detail in the handful of texts in the *Encyclopédie* on the topic. When plumbing the depths, for instance, 'Newton and Cuvier's contemporaries counted themselves lucky if they could obtain a reading from a battered instrument or collect a pinch of mud or starfish arm stuck to a plumb line that made it back to the surface.'[2] As we have all experienced, the unknown is a particularly terrifying place, making our imaginations run wild. The deep seas were imbued with astonishing emotional power from a very early point in human history. The highly complex imaginary of a part of the planet then thought to be forever beyond human reach consisted of contradictory conceptualizations that reflected both primeval chaos and the glory of God's creation. Over the centuries, the questions were always the same: were the utter, crushing darkness of the abyss, the depths devoid of the sovereignty of light, the realm of everlasting night, 'icy cold or warmed by hellfire? A pre-Creation void or teeming with life?'[3] Was there a bottom to their depth? Were they deep or shallow? Was it fair to see them as abandoned to the devil, adumbrating the chaos of the end of the world?

This mysterious, skyless realm encouraged imaginary trips into the darkness at the centre of the earth, via whirlpools draining down into the unknown. It inspired shadowy dreams. 'The ocean depths were invented before they were discovered', by means of 'descending categories [. . .] that placed the deep sea among the lairs of the impure, the abnormal, and the monstrous [. . .] the hidden, disturbing side of the world', as Jean-René Vanney writes.[4]

Twenty-first-century readers must make a concerted effort to imagine what such ignorance must have been like and the imaginary it gave rise to. The seas have lost much of their mystery for us. We have seen their depths, their topography, the astonishing creatures that live there, the methane vents and seeps scattered across the ocean floor. I remember when I visited the exhibition 'La mer, terreur et fascination' ['The sea: Terror and fascination'] at the French National Library,[5] an explorer who had descended to a depth of six thousand metres told me about the amazing sights she saw unfolding before her. She told me the first thing that struck her: 'My first thought was now I'm seeing what Plato would have so loved to see!'

The same could be said of the contemporaries of Buffon and d'Alembert. We can now all see what the deep-sea explorer saw, in films and videos that reveal the mysteries of the ocean depths, the gently swaying plants, the fascinating, beautiful creatures that dart out and catch their prey in utter silence. The realm we have come to know since 1956, when Jacques Cousteau first showed his documentary *The Silent World*, was for men and women in earlier centuries a mysterious dream-world of adventure. It is particularly crucial here for the historian to grasp the extent of the ignorance that stretched across the social spectrum.

Scholars did develop learned theories, albeit with sparse grounding in fact, based on what little information they could glean from plumbing the seas. Late-eighteenth-century thinkers often referred to Alexander the Great's brief underwater exploration with Nearchus in 334–323 BC, when the two men climbed into a primitive 'diving bell', a barrel caulked with pitch, and were lowered at the end of a cable down to the shallow coral reef off the coast of Kavran, in modern-day Pakistan. Authors also discussed astonishing designs for diving suits, wings for swimming underwater and submarines of the sort drawn by Leonardo da Vinci.

However, there was no way for them to access knowledge of anything but the shallowest seas within reach of the skilled divers who harvested sponges, as described by Herodotus. Navigators had begun using plumb lines in the seventeenth century, but almost exclusively to find safe places to anchor and to avoid becoming beached: they had little interest in exploring the scientific mysteries of the deep sea. While navigators made admirable contributions to the *horizontal* knowledge of the world, prior to the mid-nineteenth century, they did little to further an understanding of *vertical* knowledge. Between the sixteenth and eighteenth centuries, the deepest a plumb line could reach was 730 metres. The first progress came in around 1750, at the start of the period covered in this book. Academies, the great navigating companies and, later, intellectual salons began to take an interest in the ocean depths. One earlier step came in 1666, when Robert Boyle, who was a director of the East India Company as well as a leading scientist, gave orders for his ships to plumb the ocean to measure the temperature of the depths. It was of interest to scholars to find out if the deep sea was cold or if it was a source of 'caloric'.

In 1773, Captain Constantine John Phipps returned from Spitsbergen, sailing over an underwater plateau. Ordering plumb lines to be spliced together, he measured a depth to the seabed of 1,250 metres. The line brought up a small quantity of blue clay – the very first seabed sample. This marked the beginning of the 'definitive refusal to limit the knowledge of the seas to their surface'.[6]

Yet the state of knowledge remained a patchwork of learned theories and visions of the earth. Solid evidence born of careful observation was in short supply. This field, like others discussed previously, was still shaped by physico-theology and natural theology. Authors constantly harked back to a text by one of the early fathers of the church, Saint Basil, describing the blessed places God created beneath the waves. The Bible, particularly the Psalms, inspired the physico-theologians, who read Genesis for evidence of the morphogenesis of the seabed. They argued that Providence must have taken an interest in the deep seas. The vastness of the deep filled believers with devout admiration. The scholar Bernard Nieuwentijdt, a fervent Providentialist, believed that bays, capes and promontories were created by God to promote trade. It was around this time, in 1750–5, that Dr Richard Russell 'invented' what we now call the beach, sending his female patients to Brighton to bathe in the vast sea that God had, as he believed, created to heal the ills afflicting mankind. Physico-theologians and Providentialists were boundless in their admiration for God's creation: beneath the waters of the oceans, He had clearly laid out mountains and valleys populated by 'fortunate species of the abyss', more perfect still than those living on dry land. This vision of the ocean depths as a marvellous, providential space filled with living treasures[7] was eventually superseded in scientific circles, but it, together with the Biblical Flood, remained a feature of folk discourse for far longer, following the traditional belief in the 'benefits of the hidden parts of Creation'.[8]

The experimental method was little match for divine providence. Seeking to find out if there was a seabed underlying the depths, Luigi Ferdinando Marsili plumbed a continental plateau and concluded that the answer was yes; this contradicted the work of Stephen Hales, who had earlier argued – without tangible evidence – that the ocean ranged from 4,000 to 9,600 metres in depth. In fact Hales was not far from the truth, but there was no way he could prove his case. Hales was an outlier, as most scholars were reluctant to lend credence to the theory of great ocean depths, preferring the hypothesis of a relatively shallow sea. Buffon argued in 1749 that the sea was likely to be no deeper than 450 metres. The young Kant proved even further from the mark, claiming that the sea would prove to be 100 metres deep at most.[9]

I have written elsewhere of the significance of Benoît de Maillet's widely read *Telliamed* (the title being the author's name in reverse), describing a diving bell with an underwater lamp that he claimed to have used in the Indian Ocean.[10] Like Buffon, Maillet was a staunch

Neptunist. As we have seen, the leading architect of Neptunism, Abraham Werner, argued that the earth's crust was formed in the ocean depths. The geographer Philippe Buache believed that the seabed was structured by a kind of underwater framework, and drew an orographic map of what he imagined the mountainous seabed to look like. He held that the structure of the seabed consisted of mountain chains and oceanic basins. His maps were popular with scholars, who believed that the mysteries of the deep sea had at last been solved. In fact, there was very little scientific evidence in support of his theory, although his underwater orographic maps were, like Hales's theory of ocean depth, not wholly off the mark.

In truth, in the early nineteenth century, the deep sea remained, to borrow Jean-René Vanney's fine expression, 'a mysterious surface, barely scratched'.[11] A number of questions remained open: were the ocean depths warm or chilly? Were they motionless, or did currents run through them? Were they frozen in time, or did movement bring change? The first proper scientific studies of deep water only began to take place in the nineteenth century, particularly in the German-speaking area between the Rhine and the Neman rivers. Only then was the vast ignorance of deep waters reduced, as intellectual curiosity began to drive new research.

6
Discovering Mountains

Though it is doubtless an exaggeration to claim, as many historians have, that mountains did not exist as a concept prior to the eighteenth century, there is certainly a grain of truth there. As early as the fourteenth century, in 1336, Petrarch climbed Mont Ventoux for purposes that were essentially religious. A handful of humanists and scholars sometimes climbed the slopes in search of rare minerals and plants to add to their cabinets of curiosities. In 1492, Charles VIII of France ordered Antoine de Ville to ascend Mont Aiguille; the Italian wars during the reigns of Charles, Louis XII and François I cemented the vision of the Alps as a barrier defending the kingdom and of the monarchs who crossed them as heroic figures overcoming a mighty obstacle. The great Alpine military campaigns of the seventeenth century were later to reflect a similar attitude.[1]

It is nonetheless true that mountain regions remained a vast area of ignorance. What did people know about them in 1755, at the beginning of our chronology? Apart from the people living in their valleys and foothills, shepherds who led their flocks to higher pastures in the summer months, and a few pedlars and soldiers, very little. The majority of the population living in the plains, on plateaus and along the coast had never even seen them. They were doubtless spoken of occasionally, particularly in the bigger cities, as a terrifying yet awe-inspiring territory, a landscape of chaos, and above all as an obstacle.

Men of letters saw mountains as a kind of *topos horribilis*, the reverse of the *locus amoenus*, or pleasant place. Everything about them seemed inhospitable: their very appearance, their inaccessibility, violent storms and winds, and blizzards, not to mention the people who lived there, who were imagined to be wild, fierce, untamed and disturbing in physical appearance. The rare few who had personal experience of mountains described landscapes full of precipices and chasms that seemed wholly alien.

The highest peaks seemed to be lands forsaken by God and home to the devil. Their everlasting snows seemed to be a sign of their cursed nature. Another perspective, put forward by Bossuet among others, held that mountains were threatening, convulsive fragments left behind by the Flood. Even scholars had little first-hand knowledge of mountains, which remained largely unmapped, their height unmeasured. The altitudes of the Alpine summits were only determined in 1775.

A year earlier, in 1774, the geographer Pierre Martel described the summit he called Mont Blanc and worked its altitude out at 4,779 metres, which is very close to the truth (4,809 metres). The first people to explore the summits of the Pyrenees and describe them for a wider audience were military strategists.

A gradual change was under way. In the late seventeenth century, mountains became a fashionable topic of discussion among the European elite.[2] The 1729 publication of Louis Bourguet's *Théorie de la Terre*

[*Theory of the Earth*], which devoted a number of pages to mountains, helped promote the debate. The emergence of natural theology at around the same time gave rise to a new vision of mountains, particularly in John Ray's 1691 work *The Wisdom of God Manifested in the Works of the Creation*, translated into French in 1714. In the mid-eighteenth century, in 1749, the shift became more pronounced in Paul-Alexandre Dulard's long poem *La Grandeur de Dieu dans les merveilles de la nature* [*The Grandeur of God in the Marvels of Nature*]. Five years later, the Swiss pastor Élie Bertrand published an *Essai sur les usages de la montagne* [*Essay on Uses of Mountains*] which drew on Providentialism, taking mountains as an object of exploration and discovery. This led to an urge to create order from the chaos of the mountainscape, which, Bertrand argued, was merely an optical illusion. He saw mountains as nature's laboratories.

The publication of the German poet Albrecht von Haller's lengthy poem on the Alps in 1729, translated into French in 1749, made mountains highly fashionable in mainland Europe, a few years before Dr Russell sang the praises of the seashore; the English translation came some decades later, in 1794. Some elite travellers, particularly British Grand Tourists, now chose to include Switzerland and Savoy in their itineraries. As early as 1741, William Windham and Richard Pococke visited Chamonix. They became part of a new breed of Swiss tourists, begun as early as 1702–11 when the Zurich traveller Johann Jakob Scheuchzer undertook a series of excursions to the Valais, described in a lengthy book.

The mountains had been well and truly discovered – though for a long time, knowledge remained restricted to medium elevations, for instance what later geographers were to call the Prealps. In addition to new Grand Tour itineraries, several other aspects played into the discovery of the mountains at this time, including a pre-Romantic vision of Switzerland in Salomon Gessner's *Idylls* and the letter by Saint-Preux in Jean-Jacques Rousseau's *La Nouvelle Héloïse* [*New Heloise*] describing a tidy, idealized, composite Valais with all the positive attributes of mountain landscapes. The mountains described by Rousseau evoked an ideal state of nature, the world at its freshest, a new Eden.

Artists also began to produce paintings and engravings of mountainscapes, to the point where Claude Reichler has argued that knowledge of high altitudes was first and foremost iconographic in nature. Such works of art gave viewers a new sensation of sweeping vertical grandeur.

Caspar Wolf is typical of the importance of iconography in this field. His paintings, produced between 1773 and 1779, were scientific in ambition. For Claude Reichler, Wolf's works reveal his intuitive understanding of geomorphology, then a fledgling science. At that point, depictions of high mountains, 'images of both uplift and collapse', were systematically placed in the perspective of the earth's history:[3] the latent memory of the Flood or the planet's fiery origins shaped how mountains were depicted. Reichler rightly insists on the distinction between geological hypothesis and telluric fantasy – though the distinction is hard to maintain in works from this period.

A third point brought more people to mid-mountain altitudes in the latter half of the eighteenth century: the therapeutic qualities attributed to mountain air, touted in particular by the influential hygienist and doctor Théodore Tronchin, who corresponded with intellectuals all over Europe to promote his ideas. Mountain areas began to welcome people seeking what François Dagognet called the 'air cure'.[4]

Tourism began to develop in Chamonix in the 1760s. By 1785, the mountain resort already had three large inns. Visitors still came simply to enjoy the sight of the distant summits that seemed far beyond reach. The highest mountains were there to be looked at. Tourists did not attempt to climb them. Did they even want to? It seems unlikely. But by staying on lower ground, they were missing out on a range of experiences and scientific discoveries.

The highest summits remained a source of considerable fascination for some. Beginning in 1760, Horace Bénédict de Saussure spent nearly three decades travelling around the Mont Blanc massif, contemplating the mountain, analysing it from afar and imagining what it must be like to ascend it, before eventually becoming the first man to conquer its peak in 1787. He is a fine example of the power of fascination preceding a somatic experience of high altitudes. It is interesting to read his thoughts as he stood atop the Cramont – a splendid example of a powerful telluric fantasy combining the influence of Werner and Hutton, and demonstrating the significance of his expeditions before the celebrated conquest of Mont Blanc:

> Then in my mind's eye retracing the series of great revolutions our globe has undergone, I saw the sea that once covered the entire surface of the globe form, by means of deposits and successive crystallizations, first the primitive mountains, then the secondary ones; I saw those matters becoming arranged horizontally in concentric layers; and then the fire or other elastic fluids enclosed within the globe lifting and cracking that crust and bringing out the primitive inner part of that same crust, while its outer secondary

> parts remained propped on the inner layers. I then saw the waters rush headlong into chasms burst open and emptied by the explosion of the elastic fluids, and as the water rushed into the chasms, sweeping along the huge blocks we find far distant from the mountains, scattered on our plains.[5]

This was how Saussure envisioned the mountains in 1774, after, as he wrote, 'twelve or thirteen years of continual observation and reflection'.[6] The passage is incorrect in its explanation of glacial action, as we will see in a later chapter, and also contains a tacit reference to the Great Flood.

Claude Reichler sees this as a 'narrative of scientific genesis' that Saussure later dropped in favour of a theory that turned its back on Neptunism and Plutonism. However, it remains the case that in 1774, he described a powerful telluric fantasy, shared by some visitors to the lower reaches of the Alps, who felt as if they were contemplating 'the origin of the world, witnessing chaotic violence surging forth before their very eyes, at the instant of the separation of the elements'.[7]

The years 1786 and 1787 marked the first great mountaineering expeditions and the publication of their narratives.[8] From then on, a whole range of incorrect assumptions about mountains began to fade, while more accurate knowledge about them began to extend across the social scale. A full account of the richness of the discoveries arising from the conquest of the highest peaks is beyond the scope of this chapter. A few trends can be discerned, however, reflecting the new body of knowledge about mountains. Mountaineering brought a new dimension to the human gaze, which was at first destabilized by the feeling of being visually hemmed in, but then discovered the possibility of a panoptic gaze, at first vertical, then eventually panoramic. When climbers could see the world at their feet, they could identify the lie of geological strata and imagine their movement and folds – in short, travel back in time and, in Bénédict de Saussure's own words, stand in the place of God, seeing the whole world at the same time. Travellers who conquered the highest summits wrote of seeing the 'cadaver of the universe'[9] at their feet. At the same time, they experienced the visual sensation of the plunging chasm.

In the specific case of Horace Bénédict de Saussure, his writings reveal the structures and links of geology and, more broadly, an entire reading of mountain chains as laboratories of nature, the keys to a great mystery, and the solution to the enigma of earth's history. This explains an idea that quickly became a hot topic for debate: the search for the planet's highest point.[10]

In around 1800, when it became fashionable to travel to the Alps and Pyrenees, much more was known about mountain ranges than half a century previously. The birth of mountaineering had led to more in-depth knowledge, leading to a new perception and understanding of the planet as a whole. The discovery of mountains was thus a historical event of tremendous significance, ushering in a scopic revolution and an increase in cognitive capacity or, in other words, a sharp decline in ignorance.

It is important not to overstate the case. For most people, mountains remained terrifying sites of chaos and ruinous landscapes. They still seemed convulsive, disordered and self-destructive – in short, sites of catastrophe that went against the codes of natural theology in praise of God's plan. They were not beautiful; they were *sublime*. Avalanches especially were terrifying in their unpredictability. The dreadful roar and the fear of being buried alive, particularly at this time, only increased their terror. Elizabeth Woodcock wrote of being trapped under snow in 1799, hearing her husband calling for her without being able to respond, and the young Peter Salzgeber, buried for more than two days in 1807, gave an account of his dreams and visions. One well-known mountain guide, Marc-Théodore Bourrit, claimed that winter avalanches suffocated travellers without even touching them: the air pressure simply stopped them from breathing.[11]

The chill of snow, seen by some as fortifying, but more frequently as deadly, was constantly commented on. It seemed to be a manifestation of the earth's ineluctable cooling process. The Mer de Glace glacier in Chamonix seemed a vision of the future. To mountaineers and sailors on ships navigating round ice floes, cold changed the way they saw the world: its intensity roused terror and, occasionally, ecstasy. Glaciers, like lava flows, were sublime. But even in 1820, very few people living in the plains, on plateaus and along the coast had any real notion of these scientific revolutions.

7
Mysterious Glaciers

Chapter 4 discussed the debate over the nature of polar ice in the eighteenth century, pointing out that contemporaries believed the sea could not freeze over. We now turn to flows of ice in another context: glaciers. It is immediately apparent that these were an area of wholesale ignorance. No one had the least inkling of how they were formed, how they moved and what role they played in the earth's morphology. Glaciology only became established on a properly scientific footing considerably later: some argue for 1892, while Frédérique Rémy places the date earlier, in 1867 or 1868.[1] The terms 'ice floe', 'pack ice' and 'ice cap' were all in use by 1865.

More surprisingly, perhaps, the urge to fill in this blank space on the scientific map was almost totally lacking. Not until the mid-nineteenth century did anyone really try to understand how glaciers flowed or how solid bodies could change shape and extend ever further into valleys. Until this point, the Little Ice Age had seen glaciers growing. This was the final stage of their journey in the Alps. Claude Reichler writes that when travelling through the Alps, Louis Ramond de Carbonnières was haunted by a feeling that the glaciers were 'progressively invading' sites that, he believed, were under threat of coming to resemble the polar deserts, 'covering them as if with a shroud, the ice choking the upper valleys, bringing with them devastation and death'.[2]

What struck people most about glaciers, particularly in the Chamonix valley, was their advance. Shepherds harked back to 'the memory of a fortunate age when glaciers had not yet invaded the finest parts of the Alps'.[3] William Coxe saw this as the most terrifying threat to the future of the Alpine valleys. The fearsome deluge of ice threatened to engulf everything in its path. Contemporaries believed that the threat arose from the constant accumulation of ice on the highest peaks since 'the very beginning of the formation of the earth'. The advancing glaciers did not seem to follow any rules; rather, they varied according to 'capricious circumstance' – a fine euphemism for a total lack of scientific knowledge.

That said, some scholars had left their studies to take a closer look at glaciers since the 1730s. Albrecht von Haller, who almost single-handedly made mountains fashionable with his poem *Die Alpen* [*The Alps*], wrote of his astonishment at seeing ice amongst the green grass in some valleys.[4] The mid-eighteenth century, the opening of our chronological period, witnessed a shift in emotional reactions to 'glacieres', as the word was spelled for most of the eighteenth century in French and English alike until Horace Bénédict de Saussure popularized the variant 'glaciers'. The horror and fear they once provoked now turned into fascination. Their beauty, changing shape and mysterious movement were a source of wonderment as much of as incomprehension.

It had been observed that glaciers arose on mountain peaks, that the crevasses across them shifted and that they moved blocks of stone and eroded rock. The most widespread explanation was that glaciers were the result of meltwater from some vast mountaintop lake refreezing as it travelled down the slopes. But as has been seen, observation is not always enough to explain natural phenomena. This theory did not account for the ice moving. The biggest mystery was the presence of erratic blocks. One problem arose at the outset: did glaciers form from the bottom up or, as seemed more likely, from the top down? Some people suggested theories that now seem fanciful. Jean-Étienne Guettard argued in 1762 that they were the vestiges of old mountains that had eroded away completely. Jean-André Deluc claimed in 1778 that erratic blocks were the result of subterranean explosions. The most widely held belief was that they had been transported by water, or more likely mud, during floods.[5]

In parallel, as seen in the previous chapter, the Alpine glaciers were becoming a tourist attraction in their own right. They were intriguing. People wanted to get to the bottom of the mystery. There was one way of analysing them from a distance: painting them. Claude Reichler has shown the important role played by artists who painted the Alpine chasms, peaks, valleys, waterfalls and, above all, glaciers. The most famous and talented of these was Caspar Wolf. His aim was to teach people to really *see* the Alps, which he made his subject from 1773 to 1779. His ambition was as much scientific as artistic. Though he had no reliable knowledge of glacial theory, he nonetheless produced highly accurate depictions of what scholars were later to name trough valleys and morainal lakes. According to Claude Reichler, 'Eighteenth-century depictions of high mountains were always shown from the perspective of the earth's history';[6] paintings always showed mountains as convulsive. Caspar Wolf's glaciers are a case in point.

Glaciers were full of mysteries, reflecting the state of scientific ignorance that this book seeks to uncover.

8
A Fascination with Volcanoes

Grégory Quenet has conducted a valuable statistical study demonstrating that in the late eighteenth century, volcanoes took over from earthquakes as a source for scholars vainly seeking to discover the secrets of the earth's core. He writes, 'an enthusiasm for volcanoes is one of the striking characteristics of the latter half of the eighteenth century, particularly the decade from 1774 to 1784'.[1] In the 1780s, volcanoes became a fashionable topic for philosophical debate and a rich literary trope, increasingly referred to in metaphors. Yet earthquakes and volcanoes alike were still cloaked in ignorance, uncertainty and fear.

The new fashion for volcanoes arose from the extension of the aristocratic Grand Tour to the south of Italy, taking in Naples and sometimes even Sicily. The Campi Flegrei, Vesuvius and Etna were familiar to many travellers, who encountered them as tourists, strolling around them as cultural, and even to a certain extent scientific, sites of interest. Volcanoes attracted visitors awed by their majesty, admiring the marvellous spectacle, particularly at night – but they remained a mystery. The theories put forward to explain them were rather unsatisfactory, referring to the Plutonist belief in the earth's fiery core or even the Aristotelian theory of the combustion of inflammable matter in the earth's crust. While some excursionists were brave enough to explore volcanoes' flanks, most scientific observations were made from a safe distance and thus proved inadequate.

Studying volcanoes up close was difficult, for obvious reasons. A distinction can, however, be drawn between the vast majority of the population who had never even seen a volcano and the tiny minority who had seen one at first hand. The finest observers noted that active volcanoes released aqueous or acidic vapours, incandescent scoria and long 'streams of fire', or narrow ribbons of lava.

This period did, however, see the first steps in volcanology. Alexander von Humboldt argued that volcanoes are the result of the earth's core reacting against its outer crust and evidence of contact between the crust and fiery material deep within the earth. Having seen volcanoes in the Andes – a point we will return to later – he identified various categories, pointing to the multiplicity of their shapes and types of crater. He considered that the height of a volcano reflected the force that produced it, from small hills to Andean volcanic cones standing over six thousand metres in height. He pointed out that the smallest of all volcanoes, Stromboli, had been active since the days of Homer, while the tallest, towering over the Andes, went through long periods of inactivity. He also wrote that lava generally erupted from lateral openings, where the mountain's resistance was weakest; sometimes, eruptive cones formed in lateral fissures shaped like domes or beehives.[2]

It is important not to downplay the significance of references to Antiquity in the cultural background of individuals like Humboldt. Volcanoes featured regularly in texts from Antiquity, referred to as burning, vomiting, fiery mountains. The violence of volcanic phenomena led them to become personified to a great extent. Strabo was alone in giving a more accurate depiction, describing Etna's blackish smoke, incandescent blocks and lava. Cassius Dio saw the coexistence of snow and fire on volcanoes as signs of a divine presence.

In the late medieval period and the Renaissance, volcanoes once again began to feature in literature.[3] In 1495, long after Petrarch climbed Mont Ventoux, Pietro Bembo climbed Etna, where he was astonished to see a dying monster belching out fire.[4]

The seventeenth century believed that volcanoes were a gateway to the lair of the devil, Lucifer or Beelzebub. Since the days of the church fathers, and even later in scholastic thinking, they were seen as terrifying mouths of hell. Their eruptions, like many other phenomena, were fiery manifestations of God's wrath. Several authors wrote of volcanoes more like people than places or landscapes. They were alive, they died, they bore offspring: Vesuvius, which was constantly dying and reviving, became a theological mountain and a site of immortality. The unique combination of fire and snow also came to symbolize the Virgin Mary.

It is perhaps not surprising that such beliefs survived well into the eighteenth century: when Vesuvius erupted in 1779, William Hamilton recorded that the people of Naples counted on the statue of Januarius, their patron saint, and on a series of rituals to hold back the lava flowing down the volcano's flanks.

It is interesting to note the cultural references drawn on by late-eighteenth-century witnesses to volcanic activity when recording their reactions. William Hamilton carefully noted down readings from Antiquity on the question, including Strabo, Seneca, Cassius Dio, Cicero,

Tacitus and of course Pliny the Younger, who was present at the eruption of Vesuvius on 24 August 79 that killed his uncle Pliny the Elder.[5]

In addition to the extension of the Grand Tour to the south of Italy, a number of other factors played into the history of knowledge about volcanoes in the late eighteenth century. The most significant figure here is Lord William Hamilton, the British envoy to the court of the Two Sicilies, posted to Naples. He climbed Vesuvius some sixty times, including several ascensions while the volcano was erupting. On 11 May 1771, he took the Sicilian royals up Vesuvius to observe a lava flow; two years later, on 5 and 6 June 1773, he climbed Etna with Horace Bénédict de Saussure, in an interesting meeting of scientific minds.

More significantly, perhaps, Hamilton studied Stromboli. His book *Campi Phlegræi: Observations on the Volcanos of the Two Sicilies*, published simultaneously in English and French, included five letters sent to the Royal Society in London between 1766 and 1770. The book's detailed explanations, completed by fifty-four plates drawn and coloured by Peter Fabris, was the first proper scientific study of volcanic activity.

As an example, plate II shows Vesuvius erupting by night in 1779 – a relatively commonplace event – complete with a note to the effect that it was done from an original drawing produced during the eruption itself.

William Hamilton demonstrated that the Campi Flegrei were a volcanic landscape. When Vesuvius erupted from 23 December 1760 until 5 January 1761, he argued that the eruption, easily felt as far as eight miles away, must have been triggered deep inside the earth. He held that it could not possibly be a straightforward explosion of material accumulated inside the mountain, a position that was at odds with those of several other scholars, including Buffon.

Two further factors led to a more in-depth understanding of volcanoes at this time. The first of these was the wider geographical sweep of observations, due above all to the endeavours of one man: Alexander von Humboldt. From 1799 to 1804, he and his fellow traveller Aimé Bonpland led an expedition to South America, exploring the Amazon jungle, the *llanos* and the Mexican deserts. In June 1802, Humboldt climbed Chimborazo, standing over six thousand metres in height, then thought to be the world's highest peak. On his return to Europe in 1804, he wrote his *Personal Narrative of Travels to the Equinoctial Regions of the New Continent during the Years 1799–1804*, which proved wildly popular with readers and made New Spain the new focus of the natural sciences – including the study of volcanoes as sublime natural phenomena.[6]

Alexander von Humboldt's data on Andean volcanoes brought a whole new dimension to research, sidelining the volcanoes of the Mediterranean basin. Humboldt's majestic volcanoes, symbolizing the New World in their ineffable grandeur and purity of form, seemed to be the fruit of a divine epiphany. They were certainly seen as evidence of transcendence: Chimborazo was described in terms of an 'awe-inspiring, fantastical apparition [. . .] a manifestation in which nature becomes art'.[7] These volcanoes not only represented a purer form of the Sublime than in Europe, they were also signs of the alterity that seemed to characterize the New World as a whole. For Humboldt, Cotopaxi was the most regular and picturesque of all the South American peaks. At around the same time, Jean-Baptiste Bory de Saint-Vincent described the Piton de la Fournaise volcano on the Isle of Bourbon, now Réunion.

At the dawn of the nineteenth century, knowledge about volcanoes also – and indeed perhaps primarily, in terms of lived experience – stemmed from the fashion for and intensity of pictorial and, to a lesser extent, literary depictions. For cultivated individuals, volcanoes (along with hurricanes) were the natural phenomena that most stirred sensitive souls, filling them with dreadful terror and, at the same time, delight at witnessing the most spectacular display that nature had to offer. Volcanoes truly let men's souls experience the delicious terror that characterized the Sublime in the definitions of Edmund Burke and Immanuel Kant. Volcanoes also carved their own landscape and could hence be considered the finest illustration of Spinoza's concept of *Natura naturans*, or 'nature naturing'.

The grandeur and beauty of eruptions, particularly by night, the terror they aroused and the infinite power they hinted at proved inspirational for a number of British and French painters. They were not the first to take volcanoes as their subject: in the seventeenth century, when the leading theory was Athanasius Kircher's belief in earth's central fiery core, Salvator Rosa painted Etna. But it only became something of a commonplace in the eighteenth century, when many artists tackled Vesuvius erupting.[8] The Austrian painter Jacob Philipp Hackert became fascinated by Vesuvius in 1763. Among the visitors he took there were the future Tsar Paul I and Mozart. Hackert's painting of the 1774 eruption truly captures the viscosity of the magma spilling down the flanks. The artist Joseph Wright of Derby was a keen amateur geologist. He also painted Vesuvius erupting, describing the scene as the most marvellous spectacle in nature.

The most talented French painter to try his hand at the subject was without a doubt Pierre-Jacques Volaire, who settled in Naples in 1768. He was particularly fond of night scenes. Jean-Pierre Houël was one of the earliest artists to travel on to Sicily, from 1776 to 1779. His lavishly illustrated book *Voyage pittoresque des isles de Sicile, de Malte et de Lipari* [*Picturesque Travels through the Islands of Sicily, Malta, and Lipari*], published in four volumes from 1782 to 1786, is essential in understanding the history of emotional reactions to the seashore and to volcanoes. His red chalk drawing of Stromboli's crater is a highly detailed topographical study of a volcano. Inspired by his own terror, he added a comment reflecting the sublimity of his emotional response: 'Yet the horror that I felt in examining such a dreadful place was also blended with a degree of pleasure caused by the grandeur and beauty of this spectacle of fire.'[9]

The geologist and painter Jean-Pierre Houël, who travelled widely by land and sea, heralded a catastrophist vision of earth's history, foreshadowing the theses of Georges Cuvier. He saw the Lipari Islands as a great open-air laboratory, showcasing an ongoing, violent, natural revolution. It is no coincidence that the Marquis de Sade was writing at around the same time. He was fascinated by volcanic fire – he had a picture of a volcano on display in his prison cell – to the point of concluding several of his novels with volcanic eruptions and bolts of lightning, for instance *Justine ou les Malheurs de la vertu* [*Justine, or the Misfortunes of Virtue*].[10] Fashionable visits to volcanoes likewise feature in Germaine de Staël's 1807 novel *Corinne ou l'Italie* [*Corinne, or Italy*]. Knowledge about volcanoes filtered through to a broader audience by a wide range of means, from books and engravings to paintings, though it still remained restricted to a cultivated elite, the heirs to the Grand Tour tradition.

Extinct volcanoes were important to the fledgling science of geology and will be explored in greater depth in chapter 8. Here, the precursors were not William Hamilton or Jean-Pierre Houël, but Barthélemy Faujas de Saint-Fond, who wrote a 1778 study entitled *Recherches sur les volcans éteints du Vivarais et du Velay* [*Research on the Extinct Volcanoes of the Vivarais and Velay Regions*], and Jean-Étienne Guettard, a leading figure in the quarrel on the nature of basalt. Guettard was known as the 'inventor of the Auvergne volcanoes': he came up with the first classification of types of lava, ahead of his fellow geologist Déodat de Dolomieu, who also carried out fieldwork. He analysed basalt, and having initially shared Werner's belief that it was aqueous in origin, he came round to a belief in the earth's fiery core. Another significant figure was Abbot Jean-Louis Giraud-Soulavie, author of a *Histoire naturelle de la France méridionale* [*Natural History of Southern France*] in 1781 and the father of volcanic stratigraphy. He played a key role in extending knowledge of the planet's long timescale.

In the late eighteenth and early nineteenth centuries, few individuals had ever seen an active volcano, even from a distance. Among the cultivated elite of sentimental, scientific and aristocratic travellers, however, volcanoes were much more fashionable than they were to be in the later nineteenth century, when Vesuvius went through a quieter period. The same is true of earthquakes. Historians of the period have recently begun to attribute considerable importance to volcanoes, as new research throws up a host of new hypotheses. The consequences of the eruption of Laki in Iceland in 1783 and, later, Tambora were vastly more significant than could have been imagined at the time, and the 'dry fogs' of the late eighteenth century and later remained a mystery. To avoid the risk of anachronism, I will return to them in chapter 14.

It is, however, worth spending a moment looking at what was *not* known about the origins of the disaster that struck Europe in the summer of 1783, with terrible consequences. Historians have now amassed considerable data on the history of Icelandic seismology and can trace events back to the eruption of Laki beginning in June that year. The most immediate visible consequence was the arrival of what contemporaries called 'dry fogs'. It might be thought that the phenomenon is out of place in a chapter on ignorance about volcanoes. I was in fact tempted not to include them at all here, because no one at the time, except for Benjamin Franklin and two other obscure scholars, connected the two. But contemporaries did leave abundant records of what we now recognize to be the consequences of the Laki eruption.

We know, for example, that it was not the only eruption in the summer of 1783: there are records of a dozen more. The series began in Japan in December 1782 with the Iwaki eruption on Honshu and a second in the Izu archipelago. The following May, Mount Asama was the site of a massive, terrifying eruption. The sky darkened for weeks and the region was struck by famine.

In Iceland, Laki's basalt fissure became active on 8 June 1783. Lava spewed from the split for seven months. Ash and rain poured down on the crops, and the impact spread further south.[11] The mystery of what was causing the events doubtless heightened the sense of terror. Laki influenced the climate across northern Europe in the summer of 1783. Gilbert White of Selborne wrote in his diary that 'the sun, at noon, looked as black as a clouded moon, and shed a rust-coloured ferruginous light upon the ground'.[12] The fog changed colour in different times of day and places. In Laon, north of Paris, the sun shone a pale, weak orange; in the Alps, the sun was described as a 'dark red' disk that could be looked at without harming the eyes, and giving off 'bluish' light. By night, the moon and stars were barely visible. The fog that shrouded the landscape even when the sun was at its height also made the air stink of sulphur, as far south as Naples. Trees shed their leaves in June. The fog proved deadly. It was accused of causing 'putrid red fever' and spreading new diseases, particularly 'gangrenous sore throats'. The dry fog also led to dreadful storms in the summer of 1783, worst of all on 10–11 July, when the press reported children were struck down by lightning.

From this book's point of view, the main point is that the phenomenon remained unexplained. People were terrified because they had no idea what was causing it. Journals called for explanations. Readers, learning that the scourge was afflicting almost all of Europe and even parts of Asia, wrote letters sharing their astonishment and alarm. The contemporary meteorologist Louis Cotte wrote that people believed it was the end of the world. The dry fog veiling the sun led some churchmen to conclude that Doomsday was drawing near. Old folk said they had never seen or heard of anything like it. The first man to connect the phenomenon to the eruption in Iceland was said to be Benjamin Franklin, though in fact two other less well-known scholars beat him to the idea. The first was Jacques-Antoine Mourgue de Montredon, who suggested it as early as August 1783 in a paper to the Montpellier Academy, followed shortly afterwards by a Belgian Benedictine monk by the name of Robert Hickmann. Some scholars put forward other hypotheses to explain the catastrophe, such as an overflow of 'electric fluid' or an earthquake that struck Calabria and Messina on 5 February 1873. The 'dry fogs' were a source of terror for scientists as much as the rest of the population.

This episode, and the surprise and fear caused by other 'dry fogs' in the course of the nineteenth century, are further evidence of the effects of scientific ignorance, particularly when it extends across all sectors of society.

9
The Birth of Meteorology

Storms, hurricanes, cyclones, typhoons, waterspouts, violent tempests, blinding fogs: a long list of phenomena still made the earth a terrifying place, though they were increasingly accurately described. Such events swept across Europe, leading to flooding, terrible shipwrecks, and dreadful damage to property. They were part of the misfortunes of the times.

At this time, almost nothing was known about what caused them, where they came from, their paths or how to predict them. In the latter half of the eighteenth century, scholars had barely more knowledge at their fingertips than the broader population. If our goal is to understand the people who experienced such phenomena, we must take into account their lack of knowledge of atmospheric mechanisms. This was a significant factor shaping their lives.

All the phenomena that came along with great storms were well documented by mariners who sailed the farthest reaches of the ocean, in constant fear of the wrath of the heavens that could sink their ships or, more commonly, send them crashing onto rocky shores.

Storms were dramatic events that had inspired the

greatest writers and painters since Antiquity – none of whom had the slightest inkling of the atmospheric laws that caused them. They were simply attributed to Boreas or the wrath of God. However, the aim of this chapter is not to analyse the storms described by Homer, Virgil, the Acts of the Apostles, Shakespeare and Chateaubriand.

Storms and shipwrecks and their aftermath were a major theme in Enlightenment painting and literature. Such scenes were designed to arouse the viewer's empathy, allowing the artist to illustrate a range of passions, from indifference to the sublime enjoyment inherited from Antiquity and Lucretius' *suave, mari magno* ['it is pleasant, in a great sea'], or 'negative happiness'. Setting aside the long-standing Dutch tradition of seascapes for the moment, the seventeenth century ushered in a new line of marine subjects, leading to the masterpieces of Joseph Vernet, much praised by Diderot in his *Salons*, and Philip James de Loutherbourg's even more complex scenes.

Shipwrecks also featured prominently in writings from the period, from François-Thomas-Marie de Baculard d'Arnaud's serendipitous discovery of islands of untold wealth, to the tragedy of the *Saint-Géran* broken on reefs off the Island of Bourbon (now Réunion), causing the death of chaste Virginia and the despair of Paul in Bernardin de Saint-Pierre's eponymous novel. Several pages of the young François-René de Chateaubriand's *Mémoires d'outre-tombe* [*Memories from Beyond the Grave*] tell of his terrifying adventures at sea on his return from America.

Navigators and passengers alike, real or imaginary, had no way of discovering the mechanisms behind the phenomena they risked or endured. The same is true of anyone seeing a major shipwreck, in real life or in a painting.

At the same time, the 'meteorological self' was in

the ascendant – a point we will return to later – with a quest for connections between the vagaries of individuals and those of the skies. In other words, people wanted to understand how the weather affected them. Storms were of considerable emotional importance in Macpherson's Ossianism and the aesthetics of the *Sturm und Drang* movement flourishing in the German-speaking lands. The history of emotions lived, imagined, dreamed and aroused by storms, catalysing powerful emotions, mapped onto the fashion for painting storm scenes. It can be hypothesized that a lack of understanding intensified emotions, prompted dreams, and gave rise to a range of emotional responses that might have been blunted by sound scientific knowledge.

Of course, these are all examples of the aesthetic of the Sublime, in which individuals confronted nature at her wildest, experiencing both terror inspired by the sheer power unleashed and deep joy at the mere fact of existing and feeling a range of deep emotions triggered by the awe-inspiring sight. Anouchka Vasak has written of the Enlightenment 'passion for storms', when man separated from the divine to 'make the heavens and the earth his own'. The sentiment of sublimity flourished in the absence of firm scientific knowledge about storms. This was an obvious area of ignorance for the majority of the population, who had no choice but to hunker down when hit by storms they could not explain. People living along the coast had a far more extensive experience of storms than those further inland, of course. Shipwrecks long remained a common sight, arousing empathy for their victims. The huge storm that devastated great swathes of France in 1788, among others, gave those living inland some idea of the experiences of their fellow countrymen along the coast.

Like other catastrophes, storms were experienced

above all as local phenomena. The impact of a dark cloud, waterspout or hailstorm would be measured at parish level, with the hope that it would quickly move on to neighbouring areas. It is worth pointing out that while people may not have known what caused such phenomena, folk memories were long: great storms became part of the rural record, along with major floods and harsh winters.

None of this is particularly groundbreaking, but the historian must bear in mind that this dearth of knowledge was almost as widespread among scholars, including members of the Academy of Sciences. Such phenomena had not yet found rational explanations, as is clear from the great works of scientific reference from the latter half of the eighteenth century.

Not until the nineteenth century was progress made in this area, at which point knowledge became more socially differentiated. Evidence for the lack of knowledge in this area comes from a number of sources. First and foremost was the centuries-old practice of recording the daily weather, which, at the beginning of our period, revealed an ongoing focus on the harvest, trade and wars at sea. Commonplace books, diaries by members of provincial academies, aristocrats and churchmen – initially in England, then later France – recorded the weather by means of visual and somatic observation, sometimes along with data on temperature and air pressure.

Clearly, apparatus capable of accurate measurements was hard to come by at this point. Thermometers were in widespread use by the end of the eighteenth century; barometers, though invented a century earlier, remained rare. Rain gauges were scarce and rudimentary.

It is worth dwelling for a moment on the early history of the recording of meteorological phenomena, a paradoxically widespread practice given the paucity of reliable knowledge in this arena. The first fledgling attempts at scientific weather observation in the seventeenth century proved short-lived. From 1654 to 1667, Grand Duke Ferdinand II of Tuscany set up a chain of observation points across northern Italy and on towards central Europe. Records were made periodically of the wind direction, barometric pressure, degree of humidity and visibility. All the data was written down on loose paper, which was then archived.

In 1667, however, the experiment was ended under pressure from the church. At the same time, in 1660s London, Royal Society member Robert Hooke was publishing weather statistics. He dragooned his friends into helping him keep records, but they soon tired of the repetitive task and gave up. The most interesting outcome of Hooke's observations was a glossary intended to define the 'vaporous states' of the sky, but it had very little impact.[1]

In the late seventeenth century and into the eighteenth, more and more scholars began generating meteorological data sets. From 1665 to 1713, a span of almost fifty years, Louis Morin recorded the approximate daily temperature, air pressure, cloud coverage, wind direction and rainfall at the abbey of Saint-Victor south of Paris.[2]

Beginning in 1688, the French Academy of Sciences started systematically harvesting data from the Paris Observatory, publishing it from 1701 in its *Mémoires* [*Memoranda*]. Members of provincial academies then began collecting similar data. In the latter half of the eighteenth century, Louis Cotte established a vast network of correspondents across France, England and all of Europe.

One measure of the extent of scholarly ignorance in the latter half of the eighteenth century is Cotte's own *Traité de météorologie*, which claimed to represent the cutting edge of weather research. It classified weather phenomena into four categories of 'meteors': 'aerial meteors', or winds and waterspouts; 'aqueous meteors', or fog, clouds, dew, rain, frost, snow and hail; 'fiery meteors', or lightning, thunder, will-o'-the-wisps and Saint Elmo's fire; and 'luminous meteors', or rainbows and parhelia. His book reflects the age's considerable interest in weather phenomena. It is a scholarly compilation of observations, reflecting an urge to classify and categorize data. But it offers nothing in the way of explanation.

One mistaken belief that proved particularly stubborn among not only the population at large but also the scholarly elite was the idea that some weather phenomena, such as fog, emanated from the ground rather than being substances in the air, making them particularly dangerous. No one living in the latter half of the eighteenth century could read clouds or name the strange, colourful, shifting shapes drifting past overhead. Ignorance nourished their imaginations: people studying the clouds doubtless saw strange shifting scenes, mirages, fighting giants and monsters, and all manner of creatures from myths and fairy tales familiar from the cheap chapbooks sold door to door by pedlars.

Interpreting the clouds was a centuries-old practice. Men read clouds according to their own fancy. Shakespeare had Antony comment on changing interpretations of cloud shapes after his defeat at Actium: 'Sometime we see a cloud that's dragonish, / A vapor sometime like a bear or lion, / A towered citadel, a pendant rock, / A forked mountain, or blue promontory / With trees upon't that nod unto the world / And mock our eyes with air.'[3]

Later, Jonathan Swift suggested another cloud bestiary in his 1704 *Tale of a Tub*: 'there is a large cloud near the horizon in the form of a bear, another in the zenith with the head of an ass, a third to the westward with claws like a dragon'. But cloud formations are fleeting and therefore unverifiable: as Swift regretfully pointed out, they were incommunicable perceptions.[4]

This is what our forebears still saw when they gazed up at the skies in the late eighteenth century. Abbé Delille's long poem *Les Trois Règnes de la nature* [*The Three Reigns of Nature*] included a passage on reading clouds: 'The eye there sees dazzling, resplendent countrysides / Volcanoes bursting forth, mountains rising / Light striking on sparkling rocks, / Burning floods pouring from a shadowy chasm; / With rich colours and shifting shapes / Shapeless lions and steeds writhe.'[5]

The most significant factor was doubtless not knowing where atmospheric phenomena arose and the paths taken by storms, particularly at sea. No maps yet existed of their corridors, and the causes of atmospheric disturbances were a complete mystery.

Given the extent of scientific ignorance in this area, weather forecasting and steps taken to mitigate bad weather were rudimentary. Predicting the weather was a matter of folk wisdom rooted in past experience. In the countryside, weather forecasting fell to the elderly, who knew all the old proverbs. When I was a child, I knew an old farmer who would say 'Après le 15 août, adieu les beaux jours' [After 15 August, farewell to fine weather]. This proverb was grounded in past experience, and to this day many of us still remember old folk predicting rain or snow, or looking forward to an Indian summer.

That is doubtless not the main point. Weather forecasting, particularly in rural areas, was not about the seasons and proverbs. It was a somatic process based on keen-eyed sensory observation, seeing, listening, and feeling dampness on the skin. For country folk timing the harvest, it was vitally important to be able to read and feel the sky, know the meaning of each wind (which often had their own local names),[6] whether they heralded a storm or even a hurricane, and predict their consequences. Hay had to be made and wheat brought in in time to protect it from hailstorms. For centuries, such observations had anchored a local sense of place: it mattered little where such weather phenomena originated. In the absence of widespread scientific debate on the weather, that was not a question that was being asked. There were always almanacs to be consulted to decide on a preventative course of action, but their information was too vague to be of any real use locally.

Given the lack of reliable scholarly research on the weather, it is understandable that people fell back on traditional lore. Belief in divine intervention seems to have been a more powerful survival in explaining phenomena originating in the skies than in the case of earthly catastrophes. This seems logical, since they seemed to be decided at high altitudes, in the heavens depicted on Baroque cupolas, now at the feet of Mary and Jesus rather than Jupiter as had once been the case. The skies had always been associated with the divine. The clouds were God's throne. Doubts began to creep in in the Enlightenment, though this was an age rich in such depictions: there was more evidence that clouds were not solid entities or a stable infrastructure for deities to repose on.

Religious rites seeking protection from storms, hail and droughts survived until well into the twentieth century. It was widely believed for hundreds of years that inscriptions on bronze bells offered divine protection; even in the late nineteenth century, sceptics faced widespread opprobrium.[7]

It is important to identify the eighteenth-century trends

that laid the groundwork for meteorological research in the nineteenth century, filling in the blanks and institutionalizing it as a field of scholarly inquiry. First and foremost is the fascination with electricity in the latter half of the century. Benjamin Franklin's invention of the lightning rod in 1752 was the first step in taming the terror of lightning and diminishing its symbolic power. Electricity was now becoming a plaything at fashionable salons, where its marvels prompted an enthusiastic response. Scientists taming electricity helped draw lightning's terrifying sting.

The discovery of the lightning rod was an important milestone in filling in the scientific map of the skies. Franklin's invention, soon improved by the use of a pointed instrument, was taken up everywhere; France was somewhat behind the times, as such implements were first installed in Paris in 1782. As Muriel Collart writes, 'for the first time in the history of mankind, man had a means other than incantations or magic to modify a meteorological phenomenon'.[8]

Scholarly writings now occasionally began to reflect a belief that aerial phenomena and the disasters they caused had a remote origin. Alexander von Humboldt's early writings are a case in point, as is Bernardin de Saint-Pierre's 1784 *Études de la nature*, which contains a famous passage on his pleasure at hearing rain falling at night, imagining the distant lands it comes from and where it will move on to next, maybe even the Tartar steppes.[9]

The meteorological self meant looking up at the skies to follow and understand changes in the weather. This new focus and change in the human gaze, skilfully analysed by Claude Reichler, reflected an emergent attitude at the turn of the nineteenth century which played a key role in the birth of modern meteorological science.

A similar role can be attributed to the awe felt by the handful of scholars who witnessed mountain storms during the early days of Alpine mountaineering. Such powerful experiences were among the factors that could spur men on to understand the skies. To take just one example demonstrating the newness of the experience, Horace Bénédict de Saussure's *Voyage dans les Alpes* [*Alpine Journey*] describes a dramatic July storm on the col du Géant:

> An hour after midnight there arose a south-west wind of such violence that I thought that at any moment it would blow away the stone hut I and my son were lying in. [. . .] The lulls were followed by gusts of inexplicable violence. These intense gusts resembled artillery blasts: we felt the very mountain shake beneath our mattresses; the wind came in through the joints of the stone cabin, twice even lifting my sheets and blankets and freezing me from head to toe. [. . .] Towards seven in the morning, the storm was joined by constant hail and thunderbolts; one struck so close to us that we distinctly heard a spark [. . .] hissing as it slid down the wet canvas tent. [. . .] The guides, who had left the cabin, were nearly swept over the precipice. They had to cling to a rock.[10]

The new approach is clear if we bear in mind that storms were generally presented, as Anouchka Vasak writes, in terms of monsters or agents of divine wrath, in descriptions blending apocalyptic discourse and the lexicons of tragedy and technology.

This chapter earlier claimed that there was no real map of storms at sea at this point, which is true. Inland storms were, however, now being mapped. The most prominent such cartographer was the geographer Jean-Nicolas Buache (Philippe Buache's nephew), who mapped the path of the dreadful storm of 1788 across France and northern Europe, adding an accurate description of the damage the wind caused far inland: it 'swept everything up, flattened everything, dragged everything down. It whirled, tossed the clouds, twisted the trees [. . .]. It crossed deep valleys, heights, forests, and mighty rivers. [. . .]. Everything was buried, chipped up, destroyed, torn up by the roots; roofs torn away, windows smashed, cattle and sheep killed or injured.'[11] Buache's detailed map leads Anouchka Vasak to suggest that the 'great fear' of 1789 followed the same path as the storm. At this period, descriptions of storms wavered between a degree of rationality and religious and aesthetic fascination, together forming a compatible whole.

It is important to understand that at the close of the eighteenth century, it would be wrong to speak of meteorology in its modern scientific sense, even though the term itself was used by Aristotle to mean the science of the atmosphere. Works of scholarship such as Furetière's and Trévoux's dictionaries and the *Encyclopédie* did describe storms, but they made no attempt to go further and explain the phenomenon. The general lack of understanding of weather phenomena – how they arose, where they came from, their paths and mechanisms – and the absence of a commonly accepted scientific lexis, particularly for clouds, reflect a widespread state of ignorance that roused terror and fascination when storms whipped the skies. We should not let ourselves be misled by the fact that writers and painters drew on storms as themes; the depiction of powerful emotions by no means meant that ignorance was on the decline. The same was true of the mechanisms of droughts and cold snaps. In all these cases, men and women living in Enlightenment Europe in the latter half of the eighteenth century had little idea of how the world really worked.

10
Conquering the Skies

In the late eighteenth century, air, like volcanoes and electricity, was fashionable. Seeing the sky from above the clouds was a very rare privilege shared by only a handful of adventurers who had scaled the highest peaks. As early as the seventeenth century, some sought to explain their emotions as they gazed down at the clouds. One such was John Evelyn, who wrote in his diary in 1644 that it was like entering 'a most serene heaven, as if we had been above all human conversation'; this was an emotion the theatre sometimes sought to recreate.

By the 1780s, however, no one had any notion of the sensations and emotions felt when soaring high above the earth like Icarus. Here, ignorance was not merely total, but universal. The revolutionary event in this respect – perhaps the most significant of the century's closing decades, at least in terms of how the planet was represented – was the invention of manned flight in hot-air balloons, or aerostats as they were then called. A tiny number of individuals, including almost from the outset scholars equipped with measuring apparatus, experienced something humanity had been dreaming of for thousands of years. The great turning point came within the span of two years, in 1783–4.

In December 1783, not long after the Montgolfier brothers first flew a silk balloon filled with 'heated vesicular air' and Pilâtre de Rozier, together with the Marquis d'Arlandes, flew over the Château de la Muette and the Butte aux Cailles in Paris, the Robert brothers took flight from the Tuileries gardens, also in Paris. Their balloon was filled with hydrogen produced by pouring sulphuric acid onto scrap iron. This was the first piloted (vertical) flight. The event, every bit as dramatic as the first space flights in the twentieth century, took place in front of a crowd of four hundred thousand people – half of the population of Paris, making it probably the biggest crowd the world had ever seen. Subsequently, many more such experiments were conducted. Jacques Charles, one of the designers of the Robert balloon, reached an altitude of three thousand metres in the course of a two-hour flight. On his return to earth, he cried, 'I care not what the condition of the Earth is! For me, now, it is the sky. What serenity! What a ravishing scene.' At another take-off, his friends declared, 'He could hear himself living.'

The excitement spread across the channel to Britain, where continentals imported the new technology. Crowds watched in amazement as balloons took to the skies in 1784 in Edinburgh, London, Bristol and Oxford. The spectacle was celebrated in poems, songs, plays and, from 1786 on, novels. Rural areas organized receptions for people who wanted to watch balloonists such as Jean-Baptiste Blanchard, who demonstrated the technology across France. He even crossed the Channel in a balloon in January 1785 – an exploit easily as daring as Louis Blériot's first cross-Channel aeroplane flight. In the following years, endurance challenges were organized all over the world.

The adventure of flight was not limited to ballooning. André-Jacques Garnerin parachuted from a balloon tethered at an altitude of 1,000 metres in 1797; he later took advantage of the Peace of Amiens in September 1802 to jump from a balloon in London, reaching the ground ten minutes later.

At the turn of the century, such feats of derring-do made human flight not just a new experience, but also a trigger for a whole range of hitherto unknown emotions – a point we will return to – as well as a tool for scientific research and, above all, a vast public spectacle. This is a very significant point. In just a few years, an aspect of the world that no one had ever encountered was to give way to a social stratification of knowledge between the privileged few who knew what it felt like to contemplate the earth from the skies, climb to high altitudes by day or night or travel vast distances in the blink of an eye, and the vastly greater share of the population whose feet stayed firmly planted on the ground. It is often said that the nineteenth century was the age of the railway, but after the first ascension of Mont Blanc and the first balloon flight in 1783, it was also the age of the bird's-eye view, as the title of one of the most important chapters in Victor Hugo's masterpiece *Notre-Dame de Paris* [*The Hunchback of Notre-Dame*] puts it.

11

The State of Scientific Ignorance at the End of the Age of Enlightenment

Trying to forget everything you know and imagining yourself in the shoes of men and women living in the Enlightenment means thinking about how they understood our planet. This means using our modern standpoint to draw up a retrospective inventory of what they did *not* know, beliefs that we now know to be mistaken, and their fumbling steps towards the knowledge they needed to slake their *libido sciendi*.

This first part has focused largely on the latter half of the eighteenth century, the Age of the Enlightenment and the *Encyclopédie*. Thinking about how people pictured the earth, it is apparent that the map of the sciences was still largely blank. People did at least now realize that the earth was a planet orbiting the sun, that it was a sphere slightly flattened at the poles – a tangerine rather than an apple – and that its axis was inclined in relation to the ecliptic. It was also firmly established that the earth had its own history, which was extending further and further back in time.

The polar regions were to remain inaccessible for a long time to come: the vast white expanses had yet to be conquered by explorers. The earth's interior and the depths of the ocean similarly lay beyond observation, prompting bold hypotheses. Mountain peaks were just beginning to give up their secrets. Clouds drifting in the sky were as yet unnamed. Storms and hurricanes were observed and their impact felt at a local level, but their paths were unpredictable and their triggers a mystery. Nor could volcanoes and earthquakes be explained scientifically. Scholars had barely more information than in Antiquity. The age of the earth was a particularly controversial topic: had there been one Great Flood, or several? Glaciers were unexplained. Scholars were only just beginning to understand the morphology of the earth's crust, building on multiple observations driven by opposing theories.

Perhaps even more importantly, knowledge was not highly stratified in social terms. The scholarly elite was tiny in number. Their institutions and the journals that published their debates only reached a handful of people. The vast bulk of the population continued to live lives bound by the local horizon; while the earth had been partially wrested from God's grip, it remained a mysterious, terrifying place. A split was deepening between the new forms of perception and observation shared by experts, scholars, engineers, cultivated travellers and administrators, and those of ordinary people whose perceptions were shaped by their everyday lived experience and whose total lack of scientific knowledge opened the door to fear. The distinction between travellers, accustomed to thinking in terms of distance, and non-travellers, whose lives were bound by their local area, shaped the social distribution of knowledge in the latter half of the eighteenth century, as did differences in language capable of translating experiences. But for most people, vague anxieties about the world they lived in only prompted feelings of resigned despair.

How can we put ourselves into their mindset, now that we know exactly how old the earth is? We see it on our television screens ten times a day, we watch global weather reports and travel along jet streams. We know that earthquakes are disasters caused by plate tectonics, we can forecast the paths of storms, hurricanes and typhoons, and even Everest is now a rubbish-strewn tourist destination. Every day we can watch fascinating documentaries on the world beneath the waves, the marvels of the deep, the wondrous, ugly creatures that live among strange underwater plants. We see the faces of the explorers who descend to great depths.

Equatorial Africa has long since given up its secrets, the poles are opening up to tourists, and geologists use words coined over a century ago to explain the stages by which the earth's crust was formed and the movements that shaped its morphology. We know so much, and at the same time, the social stratification of knowledge has become much more pronounced. It is almost impossible to think ourselves into the mindset of our late Enlightenment forebears and imagine how they pictured the earth at a time when a revolution in feelings and emotions – in short, in sensibility – was brewing: what we learned at school to call Romanticism.

Part II

A GRADUAL DECLINE IN IGNORANCE (1800–1850)

We now leave the Enlightenment, when forward-thinking individuals aimed to combat ignorance, rid the world of preconceptions and destroy superstitions. The first part of the book showed that in terms of scientific knowledge about our planet, their achievements were somewhat limited in scope. From the dawn of the nineteenth century to the 1860s, a major turning point in the history of the West, this widespread ignorance diminished, but only slightly. Our forebears in 1850 did not know much more about the earth than their own ancestors half a century earlier. When Chateaubriand died in 1848, his mental picture of the earth had doubtless changed little since his younger days. The same can be said of the literary grandees who died in the preceding few years – Byron, Goethe, Stendhal and Wordsworth – and indeed those who were now settling into middle age, such as Flaubert, Baudelaire and Victor Hugo, not to mention the scientists whose discoveries feature in the following pages.

In many areas, the scientific map remained completely blank. No one had been able to explain the phenomenon of 'dry fogs', and the poles were to lie beyond human reach for decades to come, though some mariners did still venture to the far north and south. The same was true of the 'empty map' of equatorial Africa, and many other aspects of life on earth. Barely any progress had been made in solving the mysteries of volcanoes, earthquakes and the ocean depths. This part will therefore focus on a number of points where some progress *was* made. These include certain weather phenomena, the geological history of the earth and the fossil record. The first chapter in this part is devoted to the domain in which ignorance died back the most – the mystery of glaciation.

12
Understanding Glaciers

What was the explanation for the impressive mass of glaciers, their clearly visible shearing effect on rocks along their path, and the presence of erratic blocks that lay scattered in far distant valleys?[1] Though some timid hypotheses had been put forward in the eighteenth century, the vast majority of people, including scholars, remained ignorant of their cause. They were nonetheless much admired by artists and travellers, who shared their inexplicable marvels with a wider audience, helping reshape attitudes to nature and the enjoyment of its mysteries.

The decades from 1820 to 1840 saw a spectacular step forward in understanding the process of glaciation, leading to a radical shift in readings of the traces of temporality on the earth's surface. Ignace Venetz opened the way in 1821 by suggesting a solution to the mystery of erratic blocks found far away from glaciers. He hypothesized that the glaciers must have pushed rocks of all sizes in front of them, to the limits marked by frontal moraines. This led him to argue that glaciers must have gone through phases of expansion and shrinkage. At around the same time, Jean-Pierre Perraudin, a self-taught peasant living in the Alps, noticed scrape marks on stones trapped in the ice, which also suggested that glaciers were moving objects.

Ignace Venetz's work fell on deaf ears. His argument ran counter to the dominant theory that the planet was gradually cooling. In the late 1830s, however, the young Swiss scholar Louis Agassiz came round to his hypothesis of past periods of glaciation, given the evidence left by glacier movement. Geological observation confirmed the presence of ancient moraines, proving that glaciers had once been far more extensive than was presently the case.

On 24 July 1837, Louis Agassiz presented his theory at a meeting of the Swiss natural science society in Neuchâtel. The members found it hard to credit, particularly as he took the argument further still, applying it not just to Alpine glaciers. He pointed to the supra-regional dimension of the phenomenon and concluded that the entire planet must once have been in the grip of an 'ice age'. The argument aligned with recent discoveries and hypotheses about the fossil record. Agassiz's thesis attributed the extinction of the flora and fauna of the 'penultimate Creation' to planetary cooling.

Marc-Antoine Kaeser has written that Agassiz's identification of the traces of ancient glaciers meant the death of the old world.[2] Agassiz held that woolly mammoths must have been buried at a time when a great mass of ice covered all of northern Europe, Asia and North America; ice from the Alps must have extended as far as the city of Lyons.[3]

Agassiz's argument met with virulent opposition, not least from the greatest scholar of the age, Alexander von Humboldt. But Agassiz held firm and continued to probe the mechanisms of glacial extension. He spent the summer of 1838 with a team exploring a valley in the Bernese Oberland, then the following year around the Jungfrau and the Zermatt glacier. In 1840, he set up an open-air laboratory on the Unteraar glacier. His ambition was to answer a series of questions about the formation, composition, and structure of ice and how gravity, dilation and viscosity impacted the movement of glaciers. He devoted six years to the problem, drilling down into the ice to depths of up to some fifty metres.

The geologist Charles Lyell had already been convinced by his arguments, logically enough, as Agassiz was in fact applying his own actualist belief that past changes should be explained solely by phenomena and processes observable in the present.[4]

The Unteraar glacier quickly became famous. Tourists flocked to the site, and journals, newspapers and books all gave accounts of events there. This discredited Agassiz's opponents, turning the scholarly tide in his favour. The year 1840 saw the publication of *Études sur les glaciers* [*Studies on Glaciers*], laying the foundations for glaciology and establishing the theory of successive periods of glaciation in the Quaternary era once and for all.

The mystery had been solved. Erratic blocks – sometimes very far indeed from modern glaciers – moraines, gouge marks on rocks and trough-shaped valleys were all the result of moving glaciers. In no other field of scientific endeavour was the map filled in so spectacularly, at least for scholars and scientifically minded readers. These discoveries in glaciology further proved extremely enlightening for those who studied fossils, lending credence to Lyell's actualism, as the next chapter demonstrates.

It is hard to measure how far knowledge of Agassiz's and Lyell's theories reached in the wider population, particularly as they contradicted the belief in a single

Flood as the decisive event shaping the surface of the earth. Whatever the truth of the matter, finding answers to the mystery of the glaciers and the rise of the theory of successive periods of glaciation led many contemporaries to see the landscapes around them in a new light.

13
The Birth of Geology

The process of filling in the gaps in knowledge of the earth's history, structure and morphology from the late eighteenth century to the 1860s and identifying new approaches to reading its surface represents an extremely complex set of historical objects. This was an age when geology was beginning to take shape: it is very difficult to pin down exactly what people at the time knew and what they did not.

Three key factors came together to change geological readings of the earth at this time. The first was the long-running quarrel between catastrophism, whose most notable supporter in France was Georges Cuvier, and continuism, associated with actualism, which had been gradually gaining traction for decades before Lyell theorized it in 1830. The second is the emergence of palaeontological stratigraphy, which continues to shape the geological lexicon to the present day. The third was the ongoing debate on the globe's internal heat and the thickness of its crust.

Also present, though less immediately relevant, was the growing awareness of the extent of the 'blank spaces' of as yet unexplored territories. The Danish-French geographer Conrad Malte-Brun wrote a stinging critique of geographical ignorance.[1]

All these factors led to a fresh approach to readings of the earth, or rather landscapes, informed by the more or less clear observation of geological forms, and in some places by the new field of glaciology. These were the first timid steps towards defining what came to be known by the end of the century as 'natural regions'. A new reading of territories gradually emerged, rooted not in the historical or political past, but in geography, which now distinguished between various types of region.

This new gaze was disseminated, albeit far from systematically, by elites who set out to explore the specific geographical, ethnological and economic characteristics of various regions. This trend extended down the social scale, driven by the establishment of a new generation of scholarly societies taking a wide-ranging approach to their local surroundings.[2] Their members sought to shed light on local issues of scientific interest.

To return to the three main factors, it is important to bear in mind that in the last quarter of the eighteenth century, most scholars agreed that geological time was deep and that the history of the earth was considerably longer than the Biblical account of the Flood suggested – though this was not a view shared by the population at large. Catastrophism – a term coined by the English scientist William Whewell in 1832 – was the doctrine of those who believed that the planet was shaped by a series of major upheavals that left their mark on its surface.

One of the proponents of this theory was Georges Cuvier, who argued in 1796 at the age of twenty-seven that an earlier world had been destroyed by a catastrophe. In 1812, he expanded on his argument in his *Discours préliminaire* [*Preliminary Discourse*], followed in 1825 by his great work *Discours sur les révolutions de la surface du globe* [*Discourse on Revolutions on the Surface of the Globe*]. It argued that the earth's history consisted of a series of catastrophes, which had all led to the mass extinction of living creatures. What other explanation was there for the presence of fossil elephants (in fact, mammoths) in Siberia? Eighteenth-century thinkers had debated the question ever since the discovery of remains in a climate that was very different from their modern habitat. Bernardin de Saint-Pierre wrote a fine passage hypothesizing that the polar ice caps had once melted, causing a massive flood that swept animals from one part of the earth to another.

Cuvier based his arguments on the presence of fossils from species unknown in the modern world, which proved that catastrophes had struck the planet in succession, destroying life on earth each time. He believed that causes present in the modern world could not explain his observations: 'The thread of operations is broken. Nature has changed course, and none of the agents she employs today would have been sufficient to produce her former works.' Fossils were not, as might at first be thought, objects preserved in the earth. They were the relics of a world now lost.

The diversity of fossils extracted from the earth's strata revealed the outlines of palaeontological stratigraphy. Dating terrains by the remains found there led to the dating of successive strata, which had been identified in the eighteenth century; their history was thought to reflect the succession of marine deposits and tectonic forms. Geology was becoming a historical science, as the stratigraphic scale of fossils made it possible to identify successive events impacting the surface of the planet. Better yet, the method could be applied worldwide. There were no limits to the lexicon of palaeontological stratigraphy, based on the relative dating of strata by means of the presence or otherwise of the fossils of extinct species.

It is clear why Cuvier, though criticized by proponents of uniformitarianism and actualism, convinced eminent specialists such as Élie de Beaumont in France, Louis Agassiz in Switzerland and Adam Sedgwick in Britain. It is also worth bearing in mind that the eighteenth-century scholars Barthélemy Faujas de Saint-Fond, Horace Bénédict de Saussure and Déodat de Dolomieu had already incorporated violent events into their readings of the earth's morphology. In a previous work, I pointed out that the stratigraphy visible on cliffs along the sea front fascinated eighteenth-century thinkers, playing into the lure of the sea.[3]

Not all scientists were convinced by catastrophism, as Cuvier's theory came to be known after 1832. On the opposite side of the debate stood the actualist school and its most eminent representative, Charles Lyell, who published his *Principles of Geology* in 1830 and 1833. Lyell is one of the great names in the history of geology. He and his followers argued that the present holds the key to the past. There were no causes in the earth's history that were not still at work in the present day; in other words, the history of the globe could be read by observing actual (that is, current) causes. The actualists believed that earth's appearance had always been more or less the same. In terms of life on earth, this static vision of our planet and the understanding of time it implied went hand in hand with Lamarck's transformism. There is in fact some evidence for catastrophism in the earth's geological record, for instance the meteor strike that is believed to have wiped out the dinosaurs. However, this was not known at the time.

Significantly, paleontological stratigraphy meant terrains could be catalogued, dated and correlated over great distances. It was one of the foundational techniques of modern geology,[4] still taught to geology graduates in the twentieth century. As early as 1863, it found its way into fiction, featuring in a well-known passage in Jules Verne's *Voyage au centre de la Terre* [*Journey to the Centre of the Earth*]. It would be hard to overstate its impact on the way people thought about the surface of the earth and the layers beneath.

Another long-standing question that caused debate among scientists but went unnoticed by the majority of the population was the hypothesis that just beneath the earth's crust was a layer of molten rock. This was a major issue since, if proven, it would explain surface phenomena such as earthquakes and volcanoes and sweep aside older theories of gaseous emanations, particularly of sulphur.

No one now challenged the certainty that the earth had begun in a fluid state. Pierre-Simon Laplace confirmed Buffon's theory and the hypothesis of a gradual cooling of the globe, which caused the tectonic movements on the surface of its crust. The eminent geologist Élie de Beaumont and the physicist André-Marie Ampère saw the cooling of the globe in concentric layers as the cause not only of orogenic movements (that is, mountain formation), but also of earthquakes, volcanoes and the metamorphism of some types of rock. Most scholars of their day thought that the planet's internal heat was the main cause of the earth's current appearance.

Clearly, the first half of the nineteenth century saw improvements in the understanding of the earth, the periods of its history and movements on its surface. It is tempting to conclude that this new knowledge extended across the social spectrum. But there is little solid evidence that such scholarly debates, however heated, reached the wider population, leading to a real stratification of knowledge. Cutting-edge geological research proved difficult to explain in accessible terms and this must have limited its social impact at the lower end of the social scale. Chapter three of Flaubert's unfinished masterpiece *Bouvard et Pécuchet*, written some decades later, is one of the most scientifically informed in the whole book. Yet Flaubert nonetheless foregrounds the discrepancy between the eponymous characters' thirst for knowledge and the paucity of their real understanding in this most intellectually challenging field of the earth sciences.[5]

Similarly, reading travel accounts by some of the best-known tourists of the first half of the nineteenth century, it is striking that they show the most fervour when gazing at landscapes and heightened emotions stirred by their literary and artistic knowledge; rarely do they comment on the stratigraphy, geology or orogenesis of the regions they visit. In a word, their gazes were not yet shaped by the earth sciences, as was to become the case later in the nineteenth century and for the first half of the twentieth.

14
Volcanoes and the Mystery of 'Dry Fogs'

From late 1815 to early June 1818, the earth seemed more terrifying to the people of central and Western Europe and North America than at any time within living memory. Their terror was heightened by their utter ignorance of the mechanisms throwing the planet's natural systems into chaos.

Numerous accounts of terrifying natural phenomena survive, analysed by great minds such as Luke Howard, who applied his outstanding observational skills to the skies.[1] 'Dry fogs' veiled the earth with dark dust, to the point where the midday sun was no brighter than the moon. Seasonal temperatures went haywire and astonishingly violent storms lashed the landscape. Massive downpours caused terrible flooding from Geneva to Amsterdam and along the Rhine, swallowing up entire villages and neighbourhoods and destroying bridges. At midday on 6 November 1816, the light was so dim in Chester that lamps and candles were lit. Luke Howard recorded that on some days that month, London coachmen were forced to guide their horses through the streets. Countless crops were destroyed, leading to a major famine that caused millions of deaths, followed by epidemics including a huge outbreak of typhus.

Many people began to believe that these were portents that the end of the world was nigh. The Apocalypse seemed to be happening before their very eyes. An astronomer in Bologna predicted that the sun was dying and that life on earth was on the verge of extinction.[2] A pamphlet on sale in the streets of Paris on 17 July 1817 described the end of the world in great detail. As throughout history, processions were organized to plead for God's mercy.

No scholar could even begin to explain the disaster. However, as chapter 8 showed, this was not an entirely unknown phenomenon. In 1783, the eruption of the Icelandic volcano Laki caused similar 'dry fogs'; Benjamin Franklin was almost the only person to connect the two events. From 1815 to 1818, the causes of the terrifying darkness were even more mysterious. In fact they remained so until at least 1913, when W. J. Humphreys identified the mechanism that triggered the catastrophe. His hypothesis attracted little attention, however. When, back in the 1960s, I read up on the events of 1816, then seen by historians simply as a crisis, I had no idea what caused it. This was indeed a long-lasting area of ignorance.

Late-nineteenth-century Europeans were astounded by the scale of the eruption of Krakatoa, as we will see. But their grandfathers had never heard of Tambora, which caused such terror among the generation of 1815–18. Modern historians have foregrounded the sheer scale of the Tambora eruption and, in its light, reinterpreted the upheavals that began in 1815, took hold in 1816 and lasted until 1817. Far-reaching theories have been built on the back of the eruption: Wolfgang Behringer has controversially hypothesized that the crisis caused by Tambora led to the birth of scientific meteorology, as scholars hoped to understand phenomena that seemed inexplicable.[3] Behringer argues that well before the consequences of Tambora were identified as such, their impact on infrastructure led to major social changes: the fragility of life in the great crisis years of 1815–17 drove the creation of social policies and anti-poverty movements and led to the establishment of charitable institutions to prevent famine. Behringer goes so far as to argue that Tambora impacted popular beliefs, revived superstitions, drove an increase in anti-Semitism and even redrew the map of Europe.

His arguments may seem a stretch at times. But what is clear is the influence of the crisis on artists and writers.[4] Dry fogs influenced paintings such as Turner's *Decline of the Carthaginian Empire* (1817), Caspar David Friedrich's *Wanderer above a Sea of Fog* (1818) and a number of works by Constable.[5] The terrible darkness and storms triggered by Tambora inspired Mary Shelley in 1817 to write *Frankenstein*, described by Anouchka Vasak as a 'meteorological' novel: it also drew on recent research on the polar regions, as chapter 17 will show. Byron, Shelley and Coleridge all wrote poems about the inexplicable phenomena: men 'look'd up / With mad disquietude on the dull sky, / The pall of a past world', as Byron wrote in his 1816 poem *Darkness*.

The roots of this terror and confusion lay in ignorance of what caused such extreme events. Significantly, progress in volcanology – though the term itself had not yet been coined – was slowed by the ongoing fashion for Vesuvius and visits to the Campi Flegrei and the ruins of Herculaneum. Madame de Staël's 1807 novel *Corinne* reflects the cultural prominence of Vesuvius at the time. At the same time, the works of Alexander von Humboldt had turned his readers' attention to the volcanoes in the Andes, particularly Cotopaxi, and the volcanic peak on Tenerife.

The population at large was still fascinated by volcanoes: the late-eighteenth-century fashion showed no signs of dying out. In London, the forerunners of today's theme parks used pyrotechnic displays to simulate volcanic eruptions. Theatres in Paris and elsewhere likewise used special effects to mimic eruptions.

The few eyewitnesses to the Tambora eruption wrote official reports on the disaster, but they were read only by administrators and navy officials. They were not picked up by the news-sheets that would have described the eruption for a wider audience. In a word, Gillen d'Arcy Wood writes, the Tambora eruption was only ever described in 'notes and sketches'. One of the handful of accounts was by J. T. Ross, captain of an East India Company vessel. The *Benares* was sailing to the north of Macassar[6] on 11 April when, Ross wrote, 'The ashes now began to fall in showers. [. . .] By noon [. . .] complete darkness had covered the face of the day. [. . .] The darkness was so profound for the rest of the day, that I never saw anything equal to it in the darkest night.' When daylight eventually returned, 'the masts, rigging, decks and every part [were] covered in falling matter'.

It is worth pointing out that even had there been plenty of such accounts, we cannot be certain that the Western world would have identified Tambora as the cause of all the upheavals. We now know that this was probably the most devastating explosion of the past thousand years, and that it took place at a low latitude, making its worldwide impact much worse than if it had been closer to the pole, like Laki some decades previously.

This chapter has deliberately focused on the eruption of Tambora in Indonesia. Its aim has been to foreground the impact of ignorance, imagining ourselves in the shoes of those who experienced terrifying phenomena they could not explain. The chapter will conclude by returning to our current state of knowledge about the disaster and its worldwide impact, which could not have been analysed by those who witnessed the disasters it caused in the West at first hand. The following brief account outlines the events of the eruption, which changed the course of human history, not least closer to where it took place, in Asia.

The eruption of Tambora only lasted a few days,[7] but threw communities worldwide into chaos. On the evening of 5 April 1815, columns of smoke belched from the volcano for three hours, accompanied by a dreadful noise. Then came the cloud of black ash, rumbling and earth tremors. The following day, Tambora continued to growl and ash fell from the sky. On 10 April, the villages on the Sanggar peninsula were all wiped out as three pillars of flame spewed from the summit, sending a ball of fire hurtling down the slopes and setting the rainforest below ablaze. Boiling torrents of lava poured down the flanks. That evening, pumice hailstones rained down along with burning cinders and rain, destroying all life.

Tambora was soon cloaked with a mantle of ash and steam. A tsunami swept the coastline. For the next few days, the sun was blotted from view. The regional death toll is estimated at 100,000 people. Finally, the volcano collapsed in on itself.

Darkness reigned for two days in a radius of six hundred kilometres and a dreadful famine soon struck. Water supplies were tainted with ash, and epidemics took hold. Desperate parents killed their own children. The survivors fled to distant islands. For an entire week, the whole of south-east Asia was covered with volcanic debris. Thousands of Balinese parents tried to sell their own children for a few handfuls of rice.

Ash remained hanging in the stratosphere in the following months, creating a cloud that acted as a molecular screen for the entire planet, wrapping the earth in an aerosol film that lasted until 1818.

In the West, no one had the slightest inkling of the greatest upheaval to strike the atmosphere and the earth that century, and indeed probably that millennium. As chapter 17 shows, even the polar ice caps were affected by the Tambora eruption, leading to a new generation of Arctic exploration.

15
The Ocean Depths and the Fear of the Unknown

The first half of the nineteenth century knew little more about the depths of the ocean than the latter half of the eighteenth. Jean-René Vanney's superb study covers much of the relevant ground, mapping the extent of scientific ignorance in this domain. As we have seen in other fields of study, anyone alive in 1850 would not have known much more about the bottom of the sea than their grandparents fifty years earlier. The myths, legends and dreams of the deep studied in a previous chapter long remained anchored in their memories and imaginations, as did the framework for understanding the ocean depths. In the early nineteenth century, they were more than ever a source of what Jean-René Vanney calls 'the fear of the unknown', or of anything that lay outside their mental frame of reference. Only in the 1850s did this 'new planet' begin to come to light, as the first undersea cables were laid.

However minimal the advance of knowledge in this arena, two periods can nonetheless be identified. The first, from 1800 to 1830, corresponds to the rise and triumph of Romanticism. Artists, naturalists, botanists and writers raised public interest in the ocean depths by foregrounding the anxieties they caused.[1] The German philosophers and poets of this generation – Goethe, Schelling, Novalis – poured a torrent of new ideas, images and emotions into the ocean depths. It is worth bearing in mind that Romanticism 'lit up the mysterious path that leads to knowledge of one's inner self'. A parallel sprang up between the profundities of the soul and the ocean depths, leading to the emergence of fantastical 'abyssibility' and a 'vertical sensibility', to borrow Gaston Bachelard's expression. This leads Jean-René Vanney to conclude that 'probing the depths of the abyss and the mind emerged in a single movement'[2] – albeit with far fewer results in terms of the ocean depths.

What little progress was made came between 1830 and 1850, and can scarcely be called scientific. Sailors were constantly plumbing the depths. In most cases, their cables were too short to reach the seabed. But they were delving deeper and deeper into the ocean. Russian ships detected a depth of 1,000 metres in the Pacific. The Polar explorer James Clark Ross plumbed the ocean floor at 2,000 metres, Edward Sabine at 2,700 metres. William Scoresby plumbed 4,000 metres off the coast of Norway, at a latitude of 76° north and a longitude of 4° 5′ east. The depth of the ocean was constantly being revised, not least by scientists: the pioneering hydraulics engineer Jean-François d'Aubuisson de Voisins claimed the ocean bed must lie up to 3,600 metres beneath the surface.

At the same time, navigators brought up samples from great depths using deep-sea dredging samplers. These were small iron boxes with two jaws held open by a small peg. When the box hit the bottom, a weight closed the jaws and a sample could be brought back to the surface. James Clark Ross used such an instrument to sample the ocean floor in Baffin Bay, dredging up 'soft silt' and 'liquid mud' from a depth of 2,000 metres. Starfish were sometimes found in the samples.

Sailors did not just plumb the depths; they also used thermometers to study water temperatures far below the surface. Scoresby, Parry and many others did so by filling bottles at various depths, for instance in the chilly waters off the coast of Norway. Their measurements demonstrated that the seabed was not molten, because it did not give off great heat.

Earlier chapters discussed the quarrel between catastrophists, who followed Cuvier, and actualists, who followed Lyell. The same quarrel divided opinion on the ocean depths. Catastrophists held that the ocean floor had undergone numerous upheavals and continual reconstructions. Actualists believed that the ocean depths were a calm place, that they had always been the same as they were at present and that their sole function was sedimentation.

Jean-René Vanney argues that 1830 saw the end of a period 'in which the depths were intellectually and scientifically promoted and their value recognized and consecrated'.[3] That does not, however, mean that there was a significant reduction in scientific ignorance.

The story changed between 1830 and 1850. A proper understanding of the situation in these decades can be gleaned from two of Edgar Allan Poe's extraordinary narratives, his 1841 short story 'A Descent into the Maelstrom' and the 1838 novel *The Narrative of Arthur Gordon Pym of Nantucket*. The latter's eponymous hero and his shipmates are swallowed up by the ocean, generating visions of vast whirlpools reaching far down into the watery depths where life could not be sustained. This matched the dominant contemporary belief that the ocean depths were devoid of the teeming life found at its surface.

Scientific measurements picked up pace in these decades. Bathymetry techniques improved. In what was then known as the Ross trench, a plumb line hit bottom at a depth of 7,000 metres. Unable to explore the depths – or indeed the underwater world – in any scientific detail, researchers focused on establishing new depth records, leading to a craze for bathymetry. Samuel Haughton even estimated that the ocean might be as deep as 17,700 metres.[4]

A new research topic came into being at this time: the paths of ocean currents and their circulation far beneath the surface. Edward Forbes argued that below 550 metres, water pressure was too high to sustain life. Most people were of the same opinion: it seemed logical that life could not survive in the great depths. As a result, the impossibility of conducting proper scientific research there did not seem too much of a loss.

The long-standing belief in ancient legends recounting towns lost at sea, cathedrals swallowed up by the waves, and the magic of the deep tended to die out in cultivated circles at around this time. Diluvianism likewise gradually fell out of favour. The declining importance of maritime legends and the new imaginary space occupied by the ocean depths did not, however, have a significant impact in reducing scientific ignorance by mid-century. There was simply no way for men to explore the depths. They remained, in Jean-René Vanney's words, 'the most forsaken of all the deserts of knowledge'.[5] Their mysteries still inspired terror.

16

Reading Clouds and the Beaufort Scale

At the turn of the nineteenth century, great progress was made in understanding the textures of clouds, how they were formed and how rain fell; their shapes were categorized and given scientific labels. This filled in a large gap in our forebears' knowledge of the skies, just as the earliest aviation pioneers were experiencing them in a wholly new way.

One man single-handedly transformed the way we read the skies, sweeping away the old Baroque image of the heavens as God's throne. Luke Howard was a Quaker who spent much of his childhood lying in fields contemplating the clouds. Like many of his contemporaries, he had set up a little home weather station as early as the summer of 1788. In 1797, he joined the Askesian Society, founded the previous year by his fellow Quakers. At that time, scholars could only describe the sky and the weather in very general terms – gloomy, misty, sleety, driving, icy or snowy.[1]

One evening in December 1802, Luke Howard presented a paper at the Askesian Society that heralded the beginnings of nephology, the science of clouds. The presentation met with an enthusiastic welcome and encouragement on all sides. Weather immediately became a hot topic of conversation: Howard had suggested a new way of understanding the world. For his cultivated audience, a gap in scientific knowledge had been filled. Howard's research focused on both the mechanisms of cloud formation and their duration. His major contribution was to suggest a set of names that have survived more or less unchanged to the present. He was not the only thinker of his day to do so: the French scholar Lamarck also came up with a set of names, but it had little impact as he did not account for the process of nubification, or cloud formation.

Howard's nomenclature sorted clouds into three basic shapes, with additional categories for composite forms. He chose Latin terms, which were readily understandable by the educated elite across the West but not generally by the population at large. From highest to lowest, his general categories were cirrus, shaped like strands of fibre or hair; cumulus, heaps of black or white clouds that seemed closer to earth; and stratus, or thick layers that extended across the whole sky. There were also cumulo-stratus (which became strato-cumulus at mid-century) and nimbus, which were black clouds threatening rain. Howard's nomenclature was based not just on shape, but also on altitude, air temperature and 'the shaping powers of upward radiation'.[2] The types of clouds categorized by Howard represented various stages in the water cycle.

His nomenclature also destroyed one long-held belief that seemed rooted in common sense: the range of cloud shapes was not, as earlier descriptions had suggested, infinite. Rather, they were constant in number. The importance of this new way of understanding the skies brought meteorology into public discourse, above and beyond straightforward weather prediction. Luke

Howard explained the process of cloud formation and precipitation. Clouds formed simply when particles of water and ice rose as vapour, condensing as they reached the colder layers of the atmosphere, then falling back to earth as rain, hail or snow. In short, 'clouds form when air has risen through convection (or any other form of lifting) and has then cooled at the dewpoint'.

Howard further argued that another point was vital in understanding clouds. They are aggregates that can change shape (this was widely known, of course) and combine, thereby changing family: 'The shapes made by vapour merge and demerge, rising through convection, falling through gravity.'[3] His theory accounted for how clouds changed shape. Naming clouds therefore meant naming a series of 'evanescent forms'.

It is easy to understand why Luke Howard's explanations, suddenly plugging a major gap in knowledge, fascinated artists and poets. Several examples have been widely discussed. The first is John Constable's passion for depicting Howard's nomenclature: his *Sky Studies* of 1821 and 1822 could almost be taken for illustrations for Howard's publications. Across the Channel, Chateaubriand was similarly fascinated, while Goethe's diary for 28 April 1820 recorded both Howard's influence in Europe and Goethe's own perfect understanding of his arguments:

> Initially, one can see the cumulus, in keeping with its nature, floating at mid-altitude; when they are abundant, crenellated at their summit, paunchy in the middle, and straight-lined at their base, they move in long lines, as if placed on a layer of air. But when the cumulus rises, it is seized by the air above it, which resolves it and transfers it to the cirrus region; when it falls, it grows heavier, greyer, less able to welcome light, resting on a horizontal, oblong

> cloud base, and when it reaches the bottom, it transforms into stratus. We have seen the phenomenon produced in its greatest diversity in the semi-circle of the western part of the sky, until the heavy lower layer of clouds, attracted by the earth, was forced to fall as rain.[4]

This peerlessly precise text offers a detailed analysis, shedding light on how clouds were considered in the early nineteenth century. Howard's terminology was swiftly replacing divine or phantasmagorical visions.

Luke Howard's nomenclature and its impact on how our forebears read clouds was really the main step forward in reducing scientific ignorance of the skies in the first half of the nineteenth century. It is, however, important to be cautious in estimating how many people would have been aware of his work when looking up at the skies. To this day, my own experience of friends and family tells me that many people cannot tell a cirrus from a cumulus. Many great poets, whether they were inspired by Howard's nomenclature or simply ignored it, still read the clouds as monstrous bestiaries, fantastical cities and magical landscapes. Lengthy passages from Théophile Gautier's *Mademoiselle de Maupin* and the young Victor Hugo's poetry collection *Feuilles d'automne* [*Autumn Leaves*] are a case in point. For many people, clouds were not something they thought of in terms of scientific analysis. Rather, they were constructs that depended on the mood of the individual observing them. It would be a mistake to think that these constructs existed per se, as an objective reality outside the self.

Little else happened in the first half of the nineteenth century to fill in the scientific map of the skies. Observing weather patterns was falling out of favour among meteorologists. Fabien Locher even concludes his study of nineteenth-century weather prediction by observing widespread moral and scientific disapproval of weather forecasting in the first half of the century.[5] The practice was left to individuals such as sailors, boatmen and farm labourers, who, Horace Bénédict de Saussure noted, were better at predicting the weather than scholars, often by observing animals instinctively reacting to changes in atmospheric pressure. Forecasting also continued in traditional almanacs, along with reading the stars. However, these were scorned by scholars, who considered them as unscientific nonsense.

It may seem surprising that weather forecasting fell out of favour, given the sheer number of unusual weather events in this period, including heat waves, extreme cold snaps marking the tail end of the Little Ice Age, and dreadful storms, most notably on 6–7 January 1839 and 14 November 1845, not to mention the 'dry fogs', some caused by Tambora from 1815 to 1818 and others in 1837.

While the practice lost much of its earlier prestige and became increasingly unfashionable after 1840, many amateur weather-watchers did continue to record the local atmospheric pressure, temperature, humidity, and wind strength and direction. These were generally relatively cultivated middle-class men (or at least individuals who identified as such), including doctors, lawyers and churchmen, often playing an active role in their local scholarly societies. More broadly, the Belgian Adolphe Quételet established a long-lasting network of weather observers in 1842, while navigators, of course, continued to keep detailed weather records.

It is also striking how little scientific advances in this domain owed to the first steps in manned flight, though some balloons were indeed equipped with instruments. One exception was the work of the French scholar

Joseph-Louis Gay-Lussac, a specialist in gas chemistry. Having taken air samples at various altitudes in 1804, beating the altitude record in the process, he established that air composition was constant throughout the atmosphere.

Yet it is important not to overstate the paucity of advances in the first five decades of the nineteenth century, particularly in two domains. The first of these was the establishment of a scale for measuring wind force – a wholly new endeavour.

The mystery of where the wind came from was particularly acute. Victor Hugo wrote that his whole life long he was tortured by the enigma as he spoke to the trees and listened to them speaking in return as the wind shook their branches – the Aeolian harp beloved of the German Romantics.

'Why such whistling, always the same? Why such creaking, always the same? Why yell into the cloud to always repeat the same things?' 'What does the wind say? To whom does it speak? Who speaks to it? In whose ear does it whisper?' For Victor Hugo, the extravagances of the wind offered a special revelation of the mysteries of creation, 'the breath and call of the abyss'. Not knowing where the wind came from was a cause of suffering.[6]

The winds were indeed a mysterious presence at the turn of the nineteenth century: they had not yet found their Howard. The adjectives used to describe them remained vague and inaccurate, and more importantly, there was no way of grading their intensity. At best, people spoke of breezes, strong winds and storm winds. The last was a rather inexact term, which made it hard to identify when a storm was brewing. The only winds that people understood were the local breezes along the coast or between valleys and hillsides, which could be explained by variations in local air temperature during the course of the day. It had been known since the work of the British meteorologist George Hadley in the mid-eighteenth century that masses of air moved according to temperature changes. At a local level, folk tradition had also identified and named the winds common in the vicinity.

On 13 January 1806, four years after Luke Howard first presented his cloud categories, the Royal Navy commander Francis Beaufort was stationed in Plymouth. In his journal, he devised a classification,[7] or rather a progressive, numbered wind scale, together with appropriate orders for warships under sail. Each classification, from calm, light air and light breeze at the lower end to storm, violent storm and hurricane at the other, told sailors what to do to adapt their speed or avoid shipwreck.

By 1829, the scale was in use by most captains. In 1838, the Admiralty made it obligatory for the Royal Navy. Other scales were used alongside the Beaufort scale until the first international meteorological conference in Brussels in 1853.

The second step that improved scientific knowledge of the skies in the first half of the nineteenth century was a project to draw a dynamic map of atmospheric phenomena by means of a network of observers extending around the planet. This was a major undertaking that laid the groundwork for dynamic meteorology. In 1844, Adolphe Quételet, director of the Brussels Observatory, spoke of his ambition to use such a network to identify and map atmospheric phenomena.[8]

The research presented in this chapter was rather thin. The only real progress in filling in the scientific map of the skies in these opening decades of the nineteenth century came from Luke Howard's cloud categories and the Beaufort scale, both of which were rapidly taken up by scientists. Real progress only came just after mid-century, from 1854–5 onwards, as public opinion reacted in shock to the terrible storm that shaped the outcome of the Crimean War.

Did balloon flight teach scientists anything? What essential lessons did they learn from the sensations, emotions and impressions of manned flight? Such experiences did indeed yield some scientific results. The numerous accounts of flight by British and French aeronauts provide some useful data. First and foremost is the absence of fear: balloon flight was not seen as a terrifying, or even mildly scary, experience; it was seen as far removed from the mythical flight of Icarus, which ended when he strayed too close to the sun. The second major finding is that ballooning was not seen as some sort of sporting exploit; no deliberate attempts were made to break altitude records, for instance. The main point of interest of ballooning was being able to see the earth from above and pass through the clouds. To the end of the century, accounts regularly recorded that somatic symptoms such as breathlessness, circulation problems and sleepiness only became dangerously acute at an altitude of five thousand metres. The accounts agree on four widely shared sensations: the feeling of solitude after the frenzied activity of take-off, the unique light, the new stillness of the vast earth below, especially at night, and a strange chill.[9]

17
The Poles Remain a Mystery

Between the late eighteenth century and the discovery in 1859 of the message documenting the unfortunate John Franklin's demise twelve years earlier, very little was learned about the poles. This was in spite of numerous expeditions to the regions, most of which yielded little in the way of results, and unprecedented popular interest in the myths of the far north and south. Writers were fascinated by the poles, from Byron and Mary Shelley to Coleridge and Edgar Allan Poe, while artists sought to capture their majesty on canvas. Caspar David Friedrich's paintings of ships caught in jagged, splintered pack ice are truly spectacular.

The poles held on to their mysteries. Scholars still debated whether there was open sea at the North Pole, while Cook's claim that there was no continent of Antarctica was disputed. This chapter focuses on the Arctic and Antarctic in turn; little was known about either.

The end of the Napoleonic wars threw many British sailors out of work just as the eruption of Tambora caused a period of relatively mild temperatures in the Arctic. The years 1816 and 1817 saw exceptionally fast thaws, encouraging the British to send ships out on a new series of expeditions to find the North-West Passage. Unfortunately, the mild spell proved short-lived in the far north.

The pioneering explorer William Scoresby, captain of a whaling ship, recorded in 1817 that the Arctic seas did indeed freeze, contrary to mainstream scholarly opinion. At the same time, he noted that vast expanses of the Arctic waters were ice-free that year, which we now know was unusually warm. In 1819, John Franklin set out on his first attempt to find the passage, sailing round the Arctic for eight thousand kilometres and returning in 1822. He set out again in 1825, equally unsuccessfully.

In the meantime, John Ross set out with the *Isabella* and the *Alexander*, on a failed attempt to find the North-West Passage. In 1819, John Barrow, the driving force behind the expeditions, persuaded Ross's second in command, William Edward Parry, to set out in turn with the *Hecla* and the *Griper*. He, too, failed. Franklin's last expedition, launched in 1845 with the *Erebus* and the *Terror*, ended in one of the century's great tragedies. The ships became ice-bound; Franklin was one of the first to die, on 11 June 1847. The rest of the crew abandoned ship and set out across the ice. They all perished, with the last few survivors resorting to cannibalism before they, too, succumbed.[1]

People in Britain and elsewhere were fascinated by the loss of Franklin's expedition and the desperate hunt for survivors over the next few years. The expedition's first winter quarters were found in May 1850, and in 1854 Inuits gave accounts of seeing the unfortunate crew. The crew's final message was eventually found in 1859. A statue to Franklin, a true modern hero, was put up in central London, while the American president and the

Russian tsar lent Lady Franklin their assistance on her dogged quest for the truth.[2] Franklin's death closed a chapter, and until the end of the century, interest in the North-West Passage waned.

Though they contributed little to scientific knowledge, such dramatic events did stir the public imagination. The closing chapters of Mary Shelley's *Frankenstein*, ending with the deaths of the eponymous doctor and his monster, are set in the Arctic circle, described in all its horror and splendour. The end of the novel is voiced by Dr Walton, an idealistic polar explorer who is eventually forced to abandon his dream.

As Gillen d'Arcy Wood writes, 'the narratives of [. . .] bleak, often nightmarish journeys were devoured by millions worldwide. The bitter, gothic romance of polar exploration, first to the Arctic then to Antarctica, evolved into a defining cultural symbol of the Victorian period in Britain.' Though little was known about the poles, they remained wreathed in 'perpetual splendor',[3] a blend of terror and wonderment, that lasted until the tragic death of Captain Scott in 1912.

The poles, especially the North Pole, are a powerful symbol of this book's key argument that people at the time pictured the earth as a mysterious, terrifying place – an image born of sheer scientific ignorance.

What of the Antarctic and the South Pole in the first half of the nineteenth century? Again, science made little progress here. What information there was came above all from whalers. They were long the main source for navigators, suggesting they had a degree of recognized expertise on the region. In 1820, Tsar Alexander I sent the Russian naval officer Thaddeus Bellingshausen with his two ships, the *Vostok* and the *Mirny*, to explore the southern seas. In February, he reached 69° 25′ south, becoming the first man to see the continent that Cook believed did not exist. A decade later, in 1831, John Biscoe discovered Enderby Land, followed a year later by Adelaide Island and Graham Land. Six years later, John Balleny discovered the islands that bear his name.

In 1838, then in 1840, Britain, France and the United States all launched southern polar expeditions. Their explorers all travelled different parts of the coast of Antarctica, a land of ice that had barely been seen by human eyes. The French explorer Jules Dumont d'Urville and the American Charles Wilkes set out at almost exactly the same time. Dumont d'Urville, with his ships the *Astrolabe* and the *Zélée*, found the remains of the Lapérouse expedition, launched by Louis XVI in 1785, before landing on an island in January 1840. He christened the island, geographically part of the continent of Antarctica, Adélie, after the queen of France. Charles Wilkes also found land and gave it his own name.

These expeditions achieved little in the grand scheme. The vast continent of Antarctica, whose very existence was disputed at the beginning of the nineteenth century, offered a brief glimpse of its mysteries, and only a tiny fraction of its fringes were explored at all. As a result, the South Pole did not offer much fertile ground for the creative imagination. That is not to say that it was wholly fruitless, however. A lack of reliable knowledge may not have aroused wonderment as much as in the case of its northern sister, but generations of schoolchildren still learned Coleridge's *Rime of the Ancient Mariner* and read of the lonesome spirit 'from the land of mist and snow' at the South Pole. Similarly, Edgar Allan Poe's *Narrative of Arthur Gordon Pym*, with its descriptions of a terrifying sea dragging the hero down in a whirlpool, inspired many other writers, not least Jules Verne, whose 1897 novel *Le Sphinx des glaces*

[*The Sphinx of the Ice Fields*] was an explicit response to Poe's tale – a late-century echo of the legends of the southern oceans.

18

The State of Scientific Ignorance in the Early 1860s

By the early 1860s, Goethe, Géricault, Stendhal, Chateaubriand and Balzac were dead. The earth remained full of terrifying mysteries. Even the most cultivated contemporaries were only just beginning to understand the planet's history and geological formation. They knew nothing of the depths of the sea or what lay beneath the earth's crust, nor could they explain earthquakes and volcanoes. They could now identify and name clouds, but had not grasped the mechanisms of atmospheric circulation. The poles remained the most fascinating of the many blank spaces on the map of the world. In short, it is important to understand that from our point of view, the greatest men of letters and artists of the mid-nineteenth century would have seemed unlearned, even ignorant, about the planet they called home. The vast bulk of the population was just beginning to discover reading as an individual practice. Modern historians risk erroneous, anachronistic interpretations if they do not bear this widespread scientific ignorance in mind.

That said, the latter years of the period under study did see more scientific progress than earlier decades, though it should still not be overstated. Even in 1900, in a world that had seen two industrial revolutions, ever faster speeds that seemed to shrink distances, the almost instantaneous transmission of information, and unified time measurements, the planet remained a mysterious place in many ways. Yet rising literacy rates and scientific advances combined to increase the social stratification of knowledge.

The third part of this book will follow the previous two in considering first of all advances in knowledge of the sea, whose shallows could now be explored. The mythical submarine *Nautilus* in Jules Verne's *Vingt mille lieues sous les mers* [*Twenty Thousand Leagues under the Sea*, 1869–70] is one reflection of the urge to discover what life lay beneath the waves.

Part III

SHRINKING THE BOUNDARIES OF IGNORANCE (1860–1900)

19
Exploring the Ocean Depths

In no other area of scientific endeavour was the scientific map filled in so fast. The ocean depths were a total mystery in 1850; by the end of the century, they were a somewhat known quantity. The first discoveries came with the need to lay transatlantic cables. This meant designing equipment capable of plumbing and dredging the ocean floor and making winches that could spool out thousands of kilometres of cable. This led to new trades such as that of winchmen.[1] The process of laying cables began in the 1860s and continued to the end of the century. By 1890, 200,000 kilometres of cable criss-crossed the seabed, 350,000 kilometres fifteen years later.

Of course, this vast undertaking was driven by electrification. The American Samuel Morse invented the electric telegraph and Morse code as early as 1832: the first line, connecting Washington and Baltimore, opened in 1844. This was a genuine revolution in communication technology. Morse's system and the new transatlantic cables meant that news could now travel round the world in eighty seconds, let alone eighty days, utterly reshaping the history of curiosity, which was no longer time-bound.

It is worth dwelling on the conquest of the ocean depths for a moment. It all began with the production of a gigantic steel cable linking Britain and the United States, some 4,100 kilometres in length. Much ink was spilled at the time about the Royal Navy's groundwork and installation on the European side. The connection was made on 5–6 August 1858; Queen Victoria sent a cable to President James Buchanan.

The event garnered vast amounts of media coverage and was celebrated in poems and songs. It soon led to disappointment, however, when the connection broke down on 5 September. The ocean depths fell silent once more. Rust and wear and tear caused by the cable scraping across the ocean floor got the better of the steel. The preparations were deemed inadequate. New technology, new cables and new observations were called for.

The next step took six years. The enormous ocean liner the *Great Eastern* was pressed into service to carry the seven thousand tonnes of cable and five hundred men needed to lay it. The connection was re-established at the second attempt, on 27 July 1864. The transatlantic information superhighway was open again, and the earth seemed to have shrunk. The year 1865 marked a genuine watershed in the circulation of human thought.

However, a straightforward account of this technological triumph does not tell us how this almost instantaneous connection from shore to shore filled in the blanks in the scientific map of the ocean depths. That is another story. The first realization based on observations of the ocean bed was that Lyell was right and Cuvier was wrong. The ocean depths are a quiet world. The ocean floor was jagged and fragmented, with volcanoes here and there, but there were few sheer precipices. The ocean was plumbed to great depths over the course of these decades. As early as 1853, the crew of the

Dolphin, an American ship, located a vast 'telegraphic plateau' between Ireland and Newfoundland, three thousand kilometres long and lying at a depth of three to four thousand metres. In the Pacific, Lieutenant Brooke proved the existence of a 4,940–metre deep trench.[2] The crew of the *Tuse Arore* found a trench measuring 8,514 metres deep off the coast of Japan in 1876.

At the same time, popular science journals were teaching a wide audience about ocean currents, particularly the Gulf Stream, described by Louis Figuier in terms borrowed from the American science writer Matthew Maury as a majestic, warm, blue river flowing through the ocean: its current, he wrote, 'is more rapid than the Amazon and the Mississippi, and the mass of those two rivers represents not one thousandth part of the volume of water it carries'.[3]

The greatest discoveries involved the fauna of the deep. Descriptions of giant squid in Victor Hugo's 1866 novel *Les travailleurs de la mer* [*Toilers of the Sea*] and Jules Verne's 1870 *Vingt mille lieues sous les mers* sent shivers down readers' spines, playing into the long-standing image of the ocean depths as a monstrous, accursed place. New scientific instruments were dredging up wholly new species: some saw these as the vestiges of an archaic world and the living archive of a lost world, while for others they were life forms adapted to conditions in the ocean depths. The existence of living creatures in the deepest oceans became the great enigma of the seas.

One point of debate was whether life was also found in the very deepest trenches. In July 1869, Charles Wyville Thomson proved it did, bringing up living creatures from a depth of 4,500 metres. Mystery gave way to astonishment, but life at the bottom of the seas remained largely shrouded in mystery.

The chilly waters of the deep were another enigma, disproving the long-standing Plutonist theories. A head-spinning new hypothesis arose: might life possibly have been created in such dark, slimy places? This was a challenge indeed to the belief in God's creation.

From July 1869 on, the three-masted, steam-powered naval vessel the *Challenger*, equipped with cutting-edge scientific laboratories, improved dredging techniques and brought many new specimens to the surface. Knowledge of deep-sea fauna expanded, diversified and reached ever further beneath the waves, proving that 'all classes of invertebrates were found on the ocean floor, even large fish'.[4] It was known that species became scarcer in the lower depths. The discovery of astonishing denizens of the deep was a revolution in reducing scientific ignorance, far more so than the century's increasing familiarity with exotic wild animals: the latter had been known since Antiquity and had occasionally been shown in Europe. The new species brought up from the depths shed light on the creatures living on dry land.

In 1888, Prince Albert of Monaco showed the first collections of specimens from the deep. Four years previously, a similar exhibition had been held in Paris celebrating man's conquest of the world beneath the waves. They became a popular topic of interest by 1890, though curiously, popular science writers of the day did not dwell on them at any length. It seems that public opinion had not truly measured the significance of this great scientific leap, putting an end to thousands of years of uninformed debate.

At the same time, a major new mental framework emerged from the scientist Eduard Suess's vision of the ocean floor. He described waters cascading, the ocean floor slipping and collapsing, and a 'community of beings falling, trapped in the descent'; he believed that the earth was gradually collapsing in on itself and that humanity would witness the continents slowly yet unstoppably crumbling into the depths.[5] In a word, Eduard Suess convinced many in the late nineteenth century that all land was inevitably, and visibly, doomed to collapse. In this perspective, which echoes Spencer's *fin de siècle* pessimism, the recent exploration of the great ocean depths merely revealed that the end of the world was nigh.[6]

The science of the ocean depths did at least provide a new explanation for earthquakes and tidal waves. It became clear that they were the result of periodic collapses in the ocean floor, discrediting explanations rooted in the existence of a fiery layer beneath the crust.

At the end of the period, Jean-René Vanney writes, the ocean had been explored from top to bottom, but not by men themselves. Seabed corridors had been identified and many new species named. The ocean depths were a separate realm of life. But while this was undeniably a major step forward, its impact remained limited. Knowledge of the ocean depths does not seem to have extended far beyond specialists. It seems logical that the wider public was only interested when it was humans rather than machines doing the exploring, as indicated by the success of two novels by Jules Verne. The first, *Autour de la Lune* [*Round the Moon*, 1869], features a strange buoyant contraption equipped with portholes, with room for three scientists inside. Crashing back to earth after its lunar adventure, it falls deep into the ocean before bobbing back up to the surface. The second, perhaps Verne's best-known title, is of course *Vingt mille lieues sous les mers*, recounting the adventures of Captain Nemo and the *Nautilus*. Such imaginary submersibles, letting men travel the depths of the ocean and even explore the ocean bed freely in diving suits, truly caught the public imagination.

20
The Development of Dynamic Meteorology

Élisée Reclus's 1868 work *Histoire de la Terre* [*History of the Earth*] devoted several pages and a number of maps to the atmosphere, indicating that by this point it was seen as an integral part of the planet. Our forebears learned as much about the atmosphere as about the ocean depths in the latter half of the nineteenth century. Paradoxically, perhaps, these decades saw more terrifying descriptions of storm scenes than ever before. Jules Michelet devoted three chapters to storms in his book *La Mer* [*The Sea*], while Victor Hugo included many tremendous storms in his novels. *L'homme qui rit* [*The Man who Laughs*] opens with what is perhaps the most terrifying storm at sea in all literature. Hugo also tackled the topic in his novels *Quatre-vingt-treize* [*Ninety-Three*] and *Les Travailleurs de la mer*. Jules Verne's tales of extraordinary adventures are also full of dreadful storms; he often opens his novels with a storm, followed by a shipwreck.[1] His late novel *Le Chancellor* paints a terrifying picture of a ship adrift in a stormy sea. This was not just a French tradition: Joseph Conrad later took up the theme, making it the main 'character' in *Typhoon* (1903).

Shipwrecks were still relatively commonplace, costing countless lives. The first transatlantic liners did allay fears somewhat, at least until the disaster of the *Titanic*.[2] Along the coast, the sea remained a terrifying spectacle. The first chapter of Emile Zola's novel *La Joie de vivre* [*Zest for Life*] describes the devastation wrought on a small town on the Normandy coast when the sea flooded. On 14 November 1854, a terrible storm broke over the Black Sea, destroying some thirty British and French ships including the *Henri IV*, the pride of the French fleet. The loss was mourned across France. This came to be known as the Le Verrier storm, after the director of the Paris Observatory. A few months later, on 15 February 1855, the frigate *La Sémillante* was wrecked off Corsica, with the loss of 693 lives. These maritime disasters during the course of the Crimean campaign prompted Napoleon III to encourage meteorological research. Progress in this field was driven first and foremost by the need to make shipping safer by forecasting storms, particularly along the coast. Research was facilitated by the availability of telegraph technology, at first optical, then later by undersea cable, crucially making it possible to record and transmit the state of the sky in real time.

The initial aim, which proved decisively important, was to map air pressure and wind. In France, this was entrusted to the navy, before the Paris Observatory with its director Urbain Le Verrier began to carry out its own vital research.

The observatory established a telegraph network in June 1856 to record the weather in various locations. Before this came the symbolic date of 19 February 1855, when Le Verrier presented a report including meteorological data from across France that very day, creating a sensation among the country's numerous amateur weather-watchers. Le Verrier's telegraph network relied on a range of participants. Le Verrier and his observatory staff centralized reports from fourteen French coastal ports. Data also came in from an extensive network of keen amateurs, established from 1845 on. The network became significantly denser in the key years 1855–6. Data was recorded in many places, from amateurs' own homes to shipboard laboratories and hot-air balloons. The system gathered vast amounts of data. The minister Hippolyte Fortoul published a circular requiring teacher training colleges to collect weather data, but this met with little success until 1867, when Le Verrier asked Fortoul's successor Victor Duruy to establish a small observatory in every teacher training college across France, so that the older students could keep daily weather records. When they then took up their own teaching posts, they could teach the same techniques to their pupils. This country-wide web of data collectors provided the contents for the Paris Observatory's seven-volume *Atlas météorologique* [*Meteorological Atlas*].[3]

Mapping the sky in real time was just the first step towards the more important process of weather forecasting. Le Verrier himself tended to refer not to 'predicting' but 'warning of' the weather. Effective forecasting required a scientific understanding of how air masses moved, which in turn meant identifying and mapping atmospheric waves.

As early as 1848 in the United States and in France from 1859, the word 'cyclone' was used to refer to the circular storms that frequently hit the tropics. Edme Hippolyte Marié-Davy devoted his career at the Paris Observatory to studying atmospheric waves, working on a map of air pressure and wind. He realized that the atmosphere contained 'quasi-cyclones', which he initially called 'cyclonoids'. He mapped these, referring to them by this point as 'bourrasques' [literally 'gusts']. He studied how they arose and the paths they took. He argued that they were not, as was generally believed, cyclones that were losing their strength and dying along the coasts of Europe. Studying his maps, he saw that 'bourrasques' tended to begin in the vicinity of Newfoundland and Iceland, and to a lesser extent the Azores. This was the first proof of what are now known to meteorologists as depressions. Marié-Davy published his results in April 1866 in a work entitled *Les Mouvements de l'atmosphère et des mers considérés au point de vue de la prévision du temps* [*Movements of the Atmosphere and Seas Considered from the Point of View of Weather Forecasting*].

Three years previously, the British scientist Francis Galton had introduced the concept of anticyclones. Great strides were being made in the analysis of atmospheric circulation, leading to the birth of dynamic meteorology. In the 1880s, the concepts of masses of air and atmospheric circulation came into widespread use among meteorologists.[4]

Once again, the principal difficulty lies in establishing how far this specialist knowledge extended into the general population. One key data point is that in the late 1850s and throughout the 1860s, people across France took a keen interest in scientific weather prediction. The evening newspaper *La Patrie* [*The Fatherland*] began to print daily weather forecasts in 1858, followed in 1876 by *Le Petit Journal* [*The Little Newspaper*].

It might be thought that the rise in scientific meteorology discredited, or at least marginalized, folk knowledge in this arena. However, this proved to be far from the case. As Marié-Davy readily accepted, it was perfectly understandable that local forecasting rooted in folk memory and physical reactions to meteorological phenomena should continue.

Another form of resistance to scientific weather forecasting also proved particularly hardy, at least in France. This makes it particularly challenging to determine exactly what solid scientific knowledge people had. Scientific advances were sometimes hotly challenged by non-specialists. In this instance, an alternative form of weather forecasting, not based on physical reactions, was presented as appropriately scientific, though this was in fact far from the truth. The theories of Mathieu de la Drôme, which he disseminated in his own almanac, were taken up by countless readers across the country. His belief was that the moon was a major influence on the weather. His theories were printed in almanacs and distributed by pedlars, two major conduits for channelling information to the lower social echelons, who took up his ideas with considerable enthusiasm. In 1863, 20,000 copies of his almanac were printed just for the Seine *département*. The following year, a total of 100,000 copies were printed. The almanac long outlived Mathieu de la Drôme himself: he died in 1865. During his lifetime, his fame as a challenger to the official science was such that he even argued publicly with Urbain Le Verrier. The episode hints at the complexity of the social distribution of knowledge in terms of weather forecasting.[5] With the benefit of hindsight, it is now clear that we owe much to late-nineteenth-century science when we see daily weather maps tracking the paths of cyclones and depressions and locating anticyclones.

Another type of storm long kept scientists busy. On 28 August 1859, the eastern seaboard of the United States was lit up at length by an aurora. While the Northern Lights had long been known, it was a mystery why the phenomenon suddenly became visible as far south as the Caribbean.

A few days later, on 1 September, the astronomer Richard Carrington was observing the sun when he noticed some unusually large sunspots. At eighteen minutes past eleven, he recorded a dazzlingly bright flare emanating from one spot. This was a solar storm, which lashed the earth seventeen hours later, lighting up the entire northern hemisphere. The extremely violent event is now estimated to have destroyed as much as 5 per cent of atmospheric ozone and triggered major nitrate precipitation. The electric current of the aurora played havoc with electric circuits on earth, particularly the telegraph network. Fires broke out in a number of telegraph offices and some telegraph operators received serious electric shocks.

This solar storm and its consequences brought to light a cosmic threat to the earth's existence. Since the turn of the millennium, scientists and government authorities have increasingly turned their attention to protecting the planet from solar storms such as the one that caused what came to be known as the Carrington Event.

21

Manned Flight and the Discovery of the Troposphere and Stratosphere

Manned flight had been one of the most fascinating public spectacles since the late eighteenth century, while balloonists frequently described their unprecedented emotions at seeing the earth from above. As early as 1804, a handful of intrepid souls, such as the French scholar Gay-Lussac, soared to altitudes that then seemed terrifyingly high, to measure variations in air temperature and pressure. This marked the beginnings of high-altitude atmospheric science.

Manned flight remained a source of wonder in France and elsewhere well into the latter half of the nineteenth century, particularly in the late 1860s. Some balloon flights lasted for hours, while other 'aerial excursions' were much shorter. At this point, balloons could only be steered vertically, up or down. There was no way to manage their horizontal direction: they were simply driven by the wind.[1]

The French astronomer Camille Flammarion, himself a keen balloonist, wrote that the simple pleasure of admiring the earth from above was gradually giving way to more scientific purposes. He considered the study of the height and thickness of the atmosphere vitally important. Here he differed from the adventurers in Jules Verne's *Cinq semaines en ballon* [*Five Weeks in a Balloon*], who set out to explore the earth's surface, morphology, native peoples, flora and fauna, and cities from above.

Camille Flammarion, an outstanding popular science writer in his day, described his own impressions and emotions while ballooning: 'a strange, absolute calm, never found on earth', a striking 'sensation of immobility', no discomfort from speed, no dizziness, no feeling of acceleration or deceleration. Compared to train travel, which triggered strong emotions described in great detail by Victor Hugo as early as 1834, ballooning generated a feeling of 'sweet serenity' and an unprecedented sense of soothing calm.[2]

It is far from clear, however, that balloon flight made a major contribution in disseminating atmospheric science to a wide audience, or even to the scientific community at large. Balloon flight was above all a form of urban spectacle. Some balloonists even took paying customers up with them, promising sweeping views across the surrounding countryside as if looking down at a painting. At the end of the century, ballooning became a fairground attraction, spreading to smaller towns and even rural areas. Louis-Ferdinand Céline described the dying days of fairground ballooning in his classic novel of 1936 *Mort à crédit* [*Death on Credit*], recording the pathetic exploits of his character Courtial des Pereires, the archetypal popular science practitioner. The character puts on a short display in his patched-up old balloon every week for crowds of country folk.

To return to the salient point of this chapter, from the late 1860s on, manned flight – particularly in France – set itself new scientific objectives, gradually laying the groundwork for the study of the atmosphere.

Only some thirty years later did one crucial finding shed light on a scientific blind spot: understanding and measuring how far the earth's atmosphere extended. The closing decade of the century saw the first steps in investigating the outer layers of the atmosphere at extremely high altitudes. Léon Teisserenc de Bort, a meteorologist who specialized in clouds and atmospheric circulation, founded a private laboratory in 1892 to study dynamic meteorology, initially with a view to compiling an atlas recording the altitude and speed of clouds.[3] In 1898, at the very end of our chronology, Teisserenc de Bort began to build what he called 'kite-balloons' to maintain his instruments in position at very high altitudes. He devoted several years to studying the highest layers of the atmosphere using data from his kite-balloons, one of which achieved an altitude of twenty thousand metres.

In 1902 – a decisive date from this book's perspective – Léon Teisserenc de Bort presented his results to the French Academy of Sciences, demonstrating that between the altitudes of eight and twelve thousand metres, air temperature and pressure fell at a regular rate. Above twelve thousand metres, the data showed stability or even a slight rise. Teisserenc de Bort introduced two new words to scientific discourse: the lower atmosphere, or 'troposphere', was separated from the upper atmosphere, or 'stratosphere', by an isothermal layer. The significance of his findings is obvious, given the purpose of this book.

22

Scientific Volcanology and the Birth of Seismology

Volcanoes remained a source of fascination throughout the latter half of the nineteenth century; more than any other type of mountain, they represented an 'extreme landscape'.[1] Their supposed reach down to the planet's inner entrails made them a marvellously theatrical space that was all the more familiar since, unlike mountain peaks, they tended to be relatively accessible. Part of their power of fascination lay in accounts of disaster and the spectacular nature of eruptions that made volcanoes seem like the most dangerous places on earth. Surprisingly, the French geographer Élisée Reclus's two articles on volcanoes in the *Revue des Deux Mondes* [*Review of the Two Worlds*] in 1864–5 leave science far behind, expounding instead on the fantastical vision of mingled fire, water, air, earth and metal. He proclaimed himself struck by the volcano's power of constant metamorphosis and its ever-changing shape. Jules Michelet framed volcanoes in even more poetic terms: under their flanks beat a heart; when it faltered, the earth choked and writhed in eruptions. Lava, he wrote, was the 'blood of our Mother opening her veins for us'.[2] In Jules Verne's *Voyage au centre de la Terre*, the scientific discourse and geological content are framed in terms of ecstasy and terror. Such literary representations of volcanoes betray a lack of sound scientific knowledge, as does the geologically improbable volcano spitting flames over the frozen sea in Verne's *Aventures du capitaine Hatteras* [*Adventures of Captain Hatteras*].

Yet there were a number of advances in volcanology during this period. The first was the considerable expansion in the known geographical range of volcanoes. Vesuvius, Etna, Santorini and the other volcanoes of the Mediterranean basin, the Andes and the Canaries were joined by names from other parts of the world, arousing equal curiosity. First were the volcanoes of Kamchatka, including the highest peak in Siberia, Klyuchevskaya Sopka, standing 4,900 metres tall. Then came the Aleutian Islands, and the forty-four volcanoes of Java (jealously guarded by Dutch naturalists) including Salak and Tankuban Parahu, both highly active at that point. The most fascinating of all were the volcanoes of the Polynesian triangle, including the many volcanoes in Hawai'i. Kilauea and Mauna Kea attracted numerous travellers. The former, constantly rocked by deafening explosive activity, offered a crater lake of molten lava that was far more spectacular than Vesuvius. The 1868 explosion of Kilauea and the subsequent earth tremors entirely redrew the topography of Hawai'i.

Scientifically minded travellers had by no means forgotten about the Americas. Humboldt had not turned his attention to Mexico. Beginning in 1857, prior to and during the Second Empire military expedition, the Mexican government asked the French traveller Jules Laveirière to conduct a full-scale study of Popocatepetl, particularly Pico Mayor and the Espinazo del Diablo at its summit, with a view to observing the fissures (*respiraderos*) that spewed out sulphurous water and the *voladeros* that belched deadly gases. A second French expedition, led by Auguste Dollfus and Eugène de Mont-Serrat, drew a geological map of the volcanoes of central Mexico before moving on to El Salvador and Guatemala in 1867.[3]

Other fascinating volcanic landscapes were still being discovered. Easter Island was systematically explored in 1877, while those closer to home in Iceland were becoming more widely known. The process of exploration and research led to a list of 364 active volcanoes and a further thousand that were extinct, not including those in parts of the world beyond easy European reach in Japan and East Africa.

It was during this process of exploration, observation, description and mapping that the Indonesian volcano Krakatoa erupted at two minutes to ten in the morning on 28 August 1883. The eruption shook the world, though it was in fact far smaller in scale than Tambora had been back in 1815. The difference was that news of Tambora failed to reach Europe, and the 'dry fogs' and intense weather disruption it caused remained a mystery.

Krakatoa was quite a different story. The timing was known down to the minute, and the news spread almost instantaneously, thanks to telegraph cables under the oceans, a worldwide network of meteorological instruments and sound-level meters, and better understanding of the atmosphere. This all framed the explosion of Krakatoa in 'the planetary horizon of scientific globalization' and placed the event in 'the era of instantaneity'.[4] The whole world had access to detailed accounts of the subsequent tsunami and the atmospheric wave that was felt as far afield as Europe, as well as the composition of the volcanic ash that carried sulphur dioxide high into the upper atmosphere, diffracting the sun's rays. The long-standing mystery of what caused 'dry fogs' was now solved. Another step forward was the measurement of the decibels produced by the explosion, which was heard as far as 160 kilometres away.

Just as with Tambora, the global temperature fell, but only slightly this time. The average global temperature dropped 0.25 °C in 1884. The death toll was also far lower, though it still claimed 36,417 lives. It is an interestingly exact figure. Equally interesting was the fact that the Royal Society was able to publish a report into the local and global consequences of the explosion in 1888.

In fact, in terms of filling in the blanks of volcanology, Krakatoa was not the main event. It was perhaps the first global news story, opening a new chapter in the history of humanity, but the rapid and precise measurements that made the story worth telling were not what brought volcanic theory forward. Comparing the explosion of Krakatoa in 1883 and the Lisbon earthquake in 1755, the most significant change is in fact the analysis and dissemination of each disaster's impact.

The knowledge and understanding of volcanic mechanisms grew considerably in the latter half of the nineteenth century: for the purposes of this book, that was the decisive step. It is worth thinking a little more about what scientists had achieved. First of all, there was now unanimous agreement that volcanic matter came from deep within the earth rather than from localized fires just beneath the crust. Secondly, Leopold von Buch's theory based on his observations in the Auvergne, which had once convinced intellectual giants such as Humboldt and Élie de Beaumont, had now been discarded: no one now believed that volcanoes were uplifts caused by the pressure of underground magma.

Having analysed the history of Santorini and the Cyclades at length from 1866 on, Ferdinand Fouqué concluded that volcanic cones were the result of an accumulation of matter thrown from the crater: the volcano was, in his words, 'its own architect'. This undermined the 'craters of elevation' theory. Another French volcanologist, Charles Vélain, described the solid, liquid and gaseous 'eruptive matter' that poured, in combination or separately, from a volcano's principal crater or fissures on its base or the flanks of the cone. This led him to outline the concept of an 'eruptive model' which could change in every volcano over time.

The most decisive advance and the most fruitful theory were put forward by Ferdinand Fouqué, among others. Having realized that many volcanoes lie on or near the coast, or even at sea, he hypothesized that the earth's crust might consist of 'fields of fractures', or in other words 'fragile lines in the earth's crust' where lava could push through to the surface. Charles Vélain developed Fouqué's theory, arguing for an 'undeniable unity of volcanic phenomena' connected to the 'great dislocations affecting the earth's crust'. The science of plate tectonics was on the horizon.[5]

23
Measuring the Grip of Ice

The greatest strides in understanding the mechanisms of glaciation came in the first half of the nineteenth century, as Louis Agassiz's theories were taken up. Further progress was also made in the following decades, as demonstrated by the results of observations carried out from 1863 to 1873 in the Swiss glaciologist Daniel Dollfus-Ausset's thirteen-volume *Matériaux pour l'étude des glaciers* [*Materials for the Study of Glaciers*]. A list of the world's major glaciers, some never before identified, was gradually compiled by the end of the century, covering not just the Alps, the Pyrenees, Scandinavia and the polar regions, but also less familiar parts of the world, from the Caucasus and the southern Andes to the magnificent glaciers of New Zealand and Karakoram (now in Pakistan), where the Biafo measured a full sixty kilometres in length. Cataloguing the world's glaciers was a major undertaking: at the end of the century, they were estimated to cover a surface area of fifty thousand square kilometres.[1]

Equally significant was research into glacial periods, shaping how people read the landscape in many regions. New scholarship revealed periodical variations in glaciers and the geographical reach of periods of glaciation in earth's history. From 1854 on, scientists realized that the Chamonix glaciers were shrinking back and losing height rather than growing, as had long been feared. At the same time, their power of erosion was hotly debated: did the ice act like a plane or rather a polisher?

The most significant outcome of the research into glaciation in this half-century was the astonishing global reach of earlier glacial periods. Traces such as erratic blocks and moraines told the story of ancient glaciers,[2] demonstrating that rivers of ice once extended far into the plains and that glaciers were once found not just in the Alps and Pyrenees, but also in the Jura and Massif Central, especially the Cantal, Aubrac and Mont-Dore regions. Proof was also found that there had been two periods of glaciation in the region, and even three in the Vosges. This led Albert de Lapparent to proclaim at the end of the century that 'the grip of ice was incomparably more extensive' than had previously been thought.[3]

In 1867, Charles Martins demonstrated that the Alps and the Pyrenees had likewise undergone several periods of glaciation. Painstaking work to piece together the extent of ancient glaciers by studying gouged or polished rocks, ancient lateral moraines and erratic blocks shed light on the surface area, height and rate of melt of vanished glaciers, allowing a map of ancient glaciations to be drawn by 1880.

This explains why glaciology came into being as a new field of expertise in around 1900 in Switzerland and France. Its leading figures included the well-known scientists Jean Brunhes and Emmanuel de Martonne. Several decades of increasingly meticulous research narrowed down the timescale of ancient glaciation events and identified less immediately visible evidence of glaciation.

Detecting and mapping the fluctuations in glaciers led to a belief that the earth's climate had changed dramatically over time.[4] The planet must have warmed up between glacial periods – though by the end of the century, the reason why remained a mystery. Various hypotheses were put forward, including variations in the Gulf Stream, the intensity of the sun's rays and the increasing height of the Alps, but none of these were particularly convincing. Only much later were climate fluctuations explained, along with proof that glacial periods only existed during the Quaternary era.

It might seem astonishing at first that knowledge of advances in glaciation was more widespread than in other fields. There are two reasons for this. First, as the example of France shows, the discoveries were deliberately made accessible for a wider audience. The *Bibliothèque des Merveilles* [*Library of Marvels*] published a popular science book in 1868, *Les Glaciers* [*Glaciers*], by Frédéric Zurcher and Élie Margollé.[5] Secondly, tourism and sporting bodies took a keen interest in developments, particularly the French mountaineering club, the Club alpin français.[6]

24
Solving the Mysteries of Rivers: Fluvialism, Hydrology and Speleology

Much research has focused on the 'discovery' of mountains and the sea, the rise of mountain and coastal tourism, and the emotions they stirred. This has tended to sideline the importance of rivers and how little was known about them. They were mainly thought of as political borders that were more or less easy to cross, navigation routes, and causes of terrible floods that no one knew how to prevent.

The latter half of the nineteenth century – in fact as early as 1845, which saw the publication of Victor Hugo's major work *Le Rhin* [*The Rhine*] – saw significant contributions by geology, the new science of hydrology and, at the very end of the century, speleology. These new fields of knowledge helped shrink the boundaries of ignorance about rivers, their mysteries and the terror and wonderment they aroused.

While geologists were debating fluvialism[1] and demonstrating the importance of rivers, mapping their basins and their impact on the surrounding landscape, a number of travellers wrote of their fascination with rivers, riverbanks and estuaries. Some also sought to discover their sources. The publication of Victor Hugo's *Rhin* in 1845 is one magnificent example.

Reading the hundreds of pages of his epistolary travel narrative on the river reveals a wide range of questions about the Rhine, that, he writes, everyone visits yet no one knows. It is worth quoting him at length to understand the attraction of the river's mysteries:

> I have often told you I love rivers. Rivers convey not merely merchandise, but also ideas. Rivers are like vast clarions, singing to the ocean of the beauty of the land, the crops in the fields, the splendour of cities, and the glories of men. [. . .] Above all rivers, I love the Rhine. [When I first saw it] I contemplated at length the proud and noble river, violent yet not furious, wild yet majestic. It was in magnificent spate when I crossed it [. . .] its sound was a peaceful roar.[2]

For Victor Hugo, the Rhine was the perfect embodiment of what a river should be: 'It is swift like the Rhone; broad, like the Loire; high-banked, like the Meuse; winding, like the Seine; limpid and green, like the Somme; historical, like the Tiber; royal like the Danube; mysterious, like the Nile; spangled with gold, like an American river; and, like a river of Asia, abounding in phantoms and fables.'[3] Describing the Rhine let the poet draw up a catalogue of the earth's great rivers and their marvels and the emotions they stirred.

Hugo also discussed river activities. At Saint-Goar, he saw rafts, 'long sailing vessels', and 'small boats darting like arrows and the eight or ten steamers that regularly ply their trade up and down the river at every moment, splashing in the water like a great swimming dog, smoke pouring from their stacks and bedecked with flags'.[4] Victor Hugo was particularly interested in the source of the river, a point we will return to later. He devoted a number of lines to describing the three streams feeding into the Rhine, which join forces near Reichenau. His text reflects widespread curiosity about the phenomenon:

> A stream issues from Lake Toma, on the eastern slope of Saint Gothard; another begins in a lake at the foot of Mount Lukmanier; a third stream oozes from a glacier and descends through rocks from a height of six thousand feet. Fifteen leagues from their sources, the streams come together at a ravine near Reichenau. There, they mingle. [. . .] Three streams meet and make a river.[5]

A few years before mid-century, Victor Hugo described for his readers what hydrologists in the following decades would identify as the river's course:

> The Rhine takes on every appearance. It is at times broad, at others narrow. It is murky, clear, swift, joyous, with the great joy inherent in anything powerful. It is a torrent at Schaffhausen, a gulf at Laufen, a river at Sickingen, a great river at Mainz, a lake at Saint-Goar, a swamp at Leiden. [. . .] It grows sluggish towards the evening, as if drifting off to sleep.[6]

Since the Rhine has no resurgences, Hugo dwelled instead on the 'cataract' which for him was the most striking aspect of the river: 'it seems to me I have the Rhine Falls in my brain'; 'What a marvellous spectacle! Such a terrifying tumult! That is the first impression. Then you look at it.' Thus opens the most poetic passage in the entire book, describing the cataract, where 'gulfs are carved, filled with large white flecks [. . .] small spots of calm among the place full of horror; groves of trees mingling with the foam, charming streams meandering amidst the mossy rocks'. Then comes 'the everlasting tempest. Living, furious snow.' At the bottom, 'Black rocks sketch sinister faces beneath the foam [. . .]

Terrifying roar, awe-inspiring spate. Water becomes dust, smoke, and rain.'[7]

The emotions experienced by Élisée Reclus were no less intense when gazing on the great rivers of America, particularly when he first set eyes on the Mississippi. He lived on its shores from 1853 to 1855, considering it the simplest of rivers: 'Its source lies not [. . .] in high mountains like most (great) rivers of Europe and Asia; it does not, like the Euphrates, the Nile, or the Rhine, water landscapes celebrated in history; it is its own affair and owes nothing to history or fable.' Yet on its shores could already be heard 'the first stirrings of a great people'. Reclus foresaw that the Mississippi would become a major artery and a 'future centre of gravity for North America'.[8] Reclus, France's greatest nineteenth-century geographer, also explored the Amazon, 'the great geographic feature of the Columbian continent [. . .] Everything is colossal about this central artery of the Americas, returning to the sea vast quantities of rain and snow that fall in a basin measuring seven million square kilometres', he wrote in 1862. Unlike the Mississippi, however, its future seemed uncertain: 'This river, remarkable in the earth's history, is still almost inexistent in man's history.'[9] In terms of this book's central argument, that is exactly what makes it of interest. Reading Reclus's masterpiece *Histoire d'un ruisseau* [*History of a Stream*][10] – a title perhaps more unexpected than his *Histoire d'une montagne* [*History of a Mountain*] – it is clear that he was particularly interested in fluvialism and river sources and mouths.

Popular authors wrote about rivers just as much as the polar regions. It is often forgotten that Jules Verne described the world's great rivers as much as ice and more than volcanoes. His less well-known novels *Le*

Superbe Orénoque [*The Splendid Orinoco*] and *La Jangada* on the Amazon, the great African rivers in *Un capitaine de quinze ans* [*A Fifteen-Year-Old Captain*] and, at the end of his life, *Le Beau Danube jaune* [*The Beautiful Yellow Danube*]– of less interest than his earlier books – are no less fascinating than his best-known masterpieces. Verne's immense achievement is ripe for reassessment.

We now turn to the scientists who founded modern hydrology. For centuries, floods had been a cause of terror. They left a long folk memory, particularly in urban areas. Scholars drew up lists of floods known from earlier centuries – a scourge that they now hoped to prevent, at least in part. Engineers had long known how to build dykes and dams. Until this period, however, they had little understanding of what caused floods, attributing them simply to exceptional rainfall, either a single downpour or sustained rain over a long period. This was the new ground broken by the fledgling science of hydrology, which sought to fill in a blank space on the scientific map of rivers and explain the mechanisms of flooding.

In France, the new science was given its impetus by Napoleon III, who was deeply affected by the great floods of 1856 across much of the country, personally taking part in the relief efforts.

In July 1856, the ministries of public works and agriculture sent out a questionnaire to each *département* about its watercourses, their basins, what was thought to cause them to flood and what work was needed. The ministries were sent data on the country's four great river basins from 1860 to 1869, leading to a scientific approach to river hydrology. Numa Broc identifies 1872 as the year this new science was born.[11] The engineer Eugène Belgrand coined the term 'hydrology'. By 1878, most *départements* had their own weather and hydrology services.

Understanding river spates and floods meant doing more than merely measuring rainfall. It meant studying the geology of river basins and a set of concepts established by physical geography, including the nature and degree of ground permeability, relief and slopes, run-off intensity and the quality of vegetation. Conducting a hydrological survey meant identifying a river's source, the extent of its basin, its course, regime, tributaries, mouth and spate history.

Hydrology seemed well placed to solve long-standing mysteries about the nature of caves and chasms that swallowed up watercourses, taking rivers underground until they returned to the surface elsewhere. These mysterious underground chambers were barely explored. The aim now became to provide the answers for a series of questions, asked at the point where the new science of hydrology helped invent the new practice of speleology, or caving and potholing. Few areas of scientific endeavour saw so much progress in the closing decades of the nineteenth century.

Understanding the mysteries of how rivers behaved underground meant first and foremost conducting a series of hydrological studies into rainfall and the depth and extent of the water table, locating sources, siphons and artesian wells, and determining rock permeability to establish whether the water in underground watercourses came from infiltration, pressure, capillarity or run-off. The field was extensively theorized in 1887 in Auguste Daubrée's *Les Eaux souterraines à l'époque actuelle* [*Underground Waters in the Current Era*].

The next step was physically exploring wells, chasms, caverns and underground rivers. Daubrée had not been able to see underground rivers for himself: the first man to do so was Édouard-Alfred Martel, whose work was acclaimed far outside his native France. Martel, who founded France's Speleology Society, was a writer who excelled at making science accessible for a broad audience. His books *Les Cévennes* [*The Cevennes*, 1890] and *Les Abîmes* [*Chasms*, 1894] taught a wide readership about the circulation of underground watercourses. Martel had actually been into chasms, caverns and underground galleries to observe rivers flowing beneath the rocks before returning to the surface, entering the underground system via extant fissures in the rock.

One of Martel's major contributions was demonstrating that internal cavities arose when fractures and fissures in the rock were enlarged by a process of chemical dissolution and mechanical corrosion – in other words, by the action of water rather than successive collapses. Martel argued that underground rivers were just like those on the surface, with their own courses and even rapids and lakes.

Back on the surface, fluvialism was not just about using hydrology and meteorology to predict river spates. One centuries-old enigma with its own tinge of romance was the source of major rivers outside Europe. By the late nineteenth century, the world's great rivers had been traced back to their sources. In 1854, Burton and Speke claimed to have discovered the source of the Nile, whose regular spates had irrigated Egyptian crops for millennia. Across the continents, the blank map was filled in as explorers mapped the courses of unknown rivers and looked for the heads of major rivers. Marius Moustier and Josua Zweifel discovered the source of the Niger in 1879. More spectacularly, that same year, the sources of various tributaries of the Amazon were identified; the head of the Orinoco was found in 1886. In south-east Asia, Charles-Eudes Bonin located the source of the Red (or Hong) River in Tonkin in 1895. It is striking how relatively recent these dates are, and how long it took to fill in this blank on the scientific map.

The discovery of the source of the Mississippi is equally striking. It caused much debate until 1891, when it was generally agreed that the river did not begin at any one specific point, but rather drew its water from an extensive network of lakes.[12]

At the same time, an important chapter in the public awareness of hydrology was written when the physical geographer Paul Vidal de La Blache identified river courses as the key geographical feature structuring his vision of France. The study of French river basins became an essential aspect of French geography and knowing their sources became a form of poetic geography. Until the mid-twentieth century, French schoolchildren had to learn the names of the sources – I did so myself as a schoolboy in the 1940s. The tiny wellsprings of mighty rivers had a poetry all their own: the Loire began in Mont Gerbier-de-Jonc, the Seine in Saint-Germain-Source-Seine, the Rhône in Switzerland. Visiting the sites between 1971 and 1997, I came to realize that though they were signposted for tourists, almost no one ever came to see them. Vidal de La Blache's style of geography had long since fallen out of fashion.

25
A New Approach to Reading the Globe

The way our forebears looked at the earth around them in the latter half of the nineteenth century was informed by discoveries in geology and physical geography that shrank the boundaries of ignorance. First and foremost, geologists remained convinced that the planet was vastly more ancient than had long been thought. This period saw a number of attempts to estimate its age. This is significant, because the perception of the age of the earth proved a powerful stimulant for the imagination. In around 1900, just as radiation was being discovered, two estimations were generally accepted. The first placed the earth's age at between 20 and 25 million years, the other between 90 and 100 million. Both were far off the mark, as we now know, but these figures must be borne in mind to measure how little our ancestors just a few generations back, at the tail end of the nineteenth century, knew about the age of the earth.

The most widely accepted theory, adopted by the greatest geologists of their day including Élie de Beaumont and Eduard Suess, was that tectonic movements were the result of thermal contraction as the earth gradually cooled over the millennia, as hypothesized by Buffon.

This, it was believed, was the process driving mountain formation, volcanoes and all other tectonic phenomena, implying the presence of a layer of molten rock just beneath the earth's crust. Some scholars did argue against the idea of the earth's molten core, considering that geological forms arose instead from gradual causes and occasional accidents that remained local in scope. This controversy features in Jules Verne's *Voyage au centre de la Terre*, with Professor Lidenbrock on one side of the debate and his nephew Axel on the other.[1]

Late-nineteenth-century geologists did much to further the understanding of how mountains were formed, initially by developing more scientific methods of observation, as reflected by the work of Albert de Lapparent. They were now able to distinguish clearly between tilted, folded, overturned and fragmented strata. Geologists and physical geographers drew detailed maps of faults, fractures and all sorts of other dislocations in the earth's crust arising from uplifts, collapses and overthrusts. Eduard Suess's *Das Antlitz der Erde* [*The Face of the Earth*], published between 1883 and 1909, is a compilation of these theories.

Geologists and physical geographers began to use the term 'thrust sheet', coined by Marcel Bertrand to refer to the result of tangential movements causing terrains of different ages and types to overlap. A similar theoretical approach led James D. Dana to develop the notion of the geosyncline, or downward fold in the earth's crust, where sediment could accumulate. In terms of mountain formation, it was firmly established in 1875 that the Alps had risen on pre-existing land under pressure from the south and south-west.

Though France had had its own geographical society since 1821, physical geography was slow to become established. The most groundbreaking work was long done in Germany, thanks in no small part to Alexander von Humboldt's role in expanding Europe's geographical horizons. This went hand in hand with Conrad Malte-Brun's call, taken up by many others, for a description of all parts of the world, and with a certain frustration at the blank spaces that stubbornly remained on the world map. Countless 'universal geographies' through to the mid-twentieth century reflect the nineteenth century's ambition for encyclopedic knowledge. From the early years of the nineteenth century, Malte-Brun pointed out that knowledge of the earth was patchy, adding that he himself knew very little about Africa and nothing about Australia, where, he wrote, exploration had yet to begin.[2] This brings us back to Élisée Reclus's masterful *La Terre: Description des phénomènes de la vie du globe* [*The Earth: Description of the Phenomena of the Life of the Globe*], published in Paris in 1868, and Vidal de La Blache's 1883 work *La Terre: Géographie physique et économique: Histoire sommaire des découvertes* [*The Earth: Physical and Economic Geography: A Brief History of Discoveries*].

Physical geography had grand ambitions. It sought to incorporate aerography, hydrography and geognosy[3] and the description of all aspects of the earth's telluric surface. Physical geography made major contributions to scientific progress in the closing decades of the century, particularly in terms of three key concepts – erosion, fluvialism and cycles. Taken together with advances in glacial morphology, these made it possible to read the planet's morphology. The *Annales de géographie* [*Annals of Geography*], founded in 1891 by Vidal de La Blache, brought the most recent findings in the field to the attention of a wider audience at the turn of the century.

The aim of physical geography was to account for all

the solid forms on earth, from mountains and valleys to plains and volcanoes, to distinguish various types of mountains, and to explain surface phenomena by reading the effects of erosion. One major contributor to this new science was a series of expeditions shortly after the American Civil War to Colorado, where it was easy to read the terrain and understand how the surface had been shaped. It was a particularly clear example of denudation, which French geologists were now calling 'erosion'. They simply had to observe the lie of the land to grasp the role of erosion and dismiss catastrophism as a theory.

In 1888, Emmanuel de Margerie and Colonel Gaston de La Noë published a small work of popular science entitled *Formes du terrain* [*Forms of Terrain*], explaining that 'it was possible to understand the shape of the earth's surface by a few simple laws'.[4] The book, which argued for actualism, accounted for all types and mechanisms of erosion, from lithology (the nature of rocks) and forms of vegetation to wind action and climate change.

At the same time, fluvialism, the study of the action of rivers, was becoming a major field of scholarship and shedding light on the shape of the earth.[5] The Harvard geologist William Morris Davis presented his concept of the peneplain, increasingly discredited since 1950, and the concept of the erosion cycle.

In 1896, Albert de Lapparent brought all of these developments together in his book *Leçons de géographie physique* [*Lessons in Physical Geography*]. He took particular pains to outline the stages of the erosion cycle, from the youth of a relief to maturity to old age, possibly followed by a new phase of erosion and inversion of relief.

Physical geographers listed the various forms that

resulted from erosion, while acknowledging the particularities of volcanic, karst, glacial, aeolian and marine morphologies. In the closing years of the century, scholars had at long last grasped the sheer range of ways in which the world around us was formed. This was the outcome of many decades of thought, dating back to Horace Bénédict de Saussure's first ventures in the Alps.

Geological and geographical science came together on a smaller scale in the concept of the 'natural region', which remains relevant to this day. In France, it became a fashionable topic thanks to the *Annales de géographie*. The *Annales* themselves were the crowning achievement of a movement, particularly influential in France, which eschewed the tendency to read the national territory as a historical and political entity. This tendency had prevailed in the first half of the century, when scholarly societies were much broader in scope and interested in local phenomena. Now, late in the century, it became possible to look at the local surroundings and read them with an understanding of how the relief came to be formed. Geographers made significant efforts to teach the public at large to read space, which a select few could then correlate with its underlying geology. This was a major step forward in expanding the boundaries of knowledge about our planet. It became a less mysterious, and therefore less terrifying, place. The historian Lucien Febvre was right to underline the symbiosis between the geological structure of small regions and the nature of the community who lived in them.

26

Was There Open Sea at the Poles?

In the latter half of the nineteenth century, the scientific map of the deep seas, once a total blank, began to be filled in. The same was true of the circulation of masses of air, albeit to a lesser extent. Yet perhaps surprisingly, the state of knowledge about the polar regions remained static. Though a number of expeditions had been launched – often ending in tragedy – specialist and popular scientific discourse on the poles could only repeat stale, unproven old theories. Serious works of scholarship and the popular press alike presented vaguely diluvialist beliefs, sometimes still in the tradition of Bernardin de Saint-Pierre. People still feared an apocalyptic end to the world via 'periodical floods' caused by the melting of the polar ice caps. The myth of ice-free polar seas also recurred frequently throughout the century.

One of the most challenging mental exercises for a modern-day reader is to remember that no one in the nineteenth century had any idea what the planet looked like at the poles. Were they encrusted with a thick layer of ice? A naked plateau? Open seas? Many thought that the last hypothesis was the most likely. An entire body of polar literature was written in response to man's dream of discovering what lay at the poles. This astonishingly long-lasting gap in our knowledge, which shaped the thought of the young Joseph Conrad and Marcel Proust, among others, is fascinating to analyse: few places on earth have sparked as many flights of imagination and triggered as much public enthusiasm as the poles, which were among the last inaccessible places beyond the reach of mankind.

We left the poles in a previous chapter with the discovery of the vestiges of Franklin's expedition. The loss of Franklin and his crew was a terrifying event in the public mind, making the unfortunate explorer a folk hero. It was followed by a number of other polar expeditions, outlined here in brief. The quest for the North-West Passage was almost totally abandoned for the best part of fifty years; the few bold ventures that did set out ended in disaster. On 8 July 1879, the *New York Herald* sent George de Long and thirty-three crew members to the polar region on the *Jeannette*. The ship was crushed by shifting ice in 1881. Twenty members of the crew perished; two men were rescued by a group of Yakut hunters.[1]

On 7 July 1881, the *Proteus*, captained by Lieutenant Adolphus Greely, set sail from St John's, Newfoundland. The ship put in on Greenland, where the crew was joined by the French doctor Octave Pavy. The terrible weather conditions forced the entire crew to take to a lifeboat on 29 July 1883. All but seven of the men died. Greely was one of the fortunate survivors to be picked up by a sealing ship. As had been the case for the Franklin expedition, when the bodies were recovered, they bore traces of cannibalism.

The best-known of the navigators to set out to find open waters at the North Pole was the Norwegian

Fridtjof Nansen. He left Bergen with a team of twelve men and thirty-four dogs on 24 June 1893, aboard the *Fram*. He had designed the ship himself, with a specially rounded hull to withstand ice pressure. The expedition ended in failure, as did a second attempt in 1895.[2] Though many did still believe at this point that open waters would be found at the pole, by the end of the century it was increasingly clear that the sea at the North Pole was frozen.

Several attempts to reach the North Pole by hot-air balloon also came to nothing. In 1896, the Swedish engineer Salomon Andrée made the first attempt in a balloon made in Paris, with the support of the king of Sweden and Alfred Nobel. When that attempt failed, Andrée tried again in 1897 with the engineer Knut Fraenkel and the photographer Nils Strindberg. The balloon was forced to land on pack ice; the three heroes tried to walk to safety, surviving for two months on bear meat before eventually succumbing to the elements.[3]

Adolf Nordenskiöld proved more fortunate on his quest to locate the North-East Passage. He set sail from Gothenburg, Sweden, on 4 July 1878 with two ships, the *Vega* and the *Lena*. He spent the first winter sheltering with the Chukchi people. The *Vega* eventually broke free from the ice in 1879 and made it through, reaching Yokohama on 2 September, to a rapturous reception from the Japanese. The navigator was later given a hero's welcome in Paris by the French president and Victor Hugo.

The Antarctic was explored for a year in 1897, but it remained on the sidelines of science for five decades, compared to the flurry of interest earlier in the century.

The sheer inaccessibility of the poles, demonstrated by the failure of numerous expeditions over the centuries, sparked the public imagination. Widespread fascination with the poles and the vast outpouring of books on the ice caps were driven by failure and an ongoing dearth of knowledge. The same was true of two scientific theories that are relevant here, the first as a cultural relic, the second as the ultimate phase of an idyllic myth.

As early as 1842, Joseph Adhémar hypothesized that the accumulation of ice at one of the poles must lead to a great flood between the hemispheres every 10,500 years.[4] His theory reveals the influence of Bernardin de Saint-Pierre's magnificent description of Noah's Flood in *Études de la nature*. Adhémar's theory remained influential for decades, with followers including Henri-Sébastien Le Hon and Paul de Jouvancel. In 1860, Le Hon predicted a cataclysm would take place in AD 7860.[5] He proposed rebuilding Paris on top of the Massif Central to avoid flooding. Society would be forced to adapt by producing artificial suns and floating cities, then move en masse to the southern hemisphere, before eventually becoming extinct. The Fourierist Adolphe Alhaiza, a devotee of Adhémar, published *Cybèle: Voyage extraordinaire dans l'avenir* [*Cybele: An Extraordinary Trip to the Future*] in 1891 using the pseudonym Jean Chambon. It claimed similarly that by AD 7248, the waters of the southern ice cap would cover Europe entirely.[6]

The thinking of Paul de Jouvancel on periodical flooding was even more influential.[7] The year 1861 saw the publication of his own vision of the future catastrophe, building on Adhémar: *Les Déluges: Développement du globe et de l'organisation géologique* [*Floods: Development of the Globe and of Geological Organization*]. The title reflects the scale of the author's scientific ambition. Taking Buffon's theory of the gradually cooling earth as his starting point, he calculated that the poles cooled down in turn every 10,500 years. The end of each cycle triggered a terrible disaster, as the vast quantity of ice accumulated in one of the polar regions collapsed into the sea, causing a massive tsunami that tore up mountains, devastated forests, drowned animals and churned up the ocean depths. The earth would then regenerate until the next disaster from the other end of the planet, 10,500 years later.

Such theories reached a wide audience, causing a newly scientific strain of terror that replaced the Biblical fear of divine retribution by flooding. Several journals featured articles on the theory of periodical flooding, including the widely read *Magasin pittoresque* [*Picturesque Store*] in 1881. Even such an established scholar as Alfred Maury lent support to Adhémar's theory in 1860.

The fascinating, ancient belief in open water at the poles proved to stir the public imagination even more than periodical flooding. The idea gained new credence in 1859, or even as early as 1853, when the remains of Franklin's expedition were found. It was as if the horror of that disaster gave rise to the need for an idyllic myth to make up for it. The new myth proved particularly powerful in Germany, as well as in Britain, France and the United States to a lesser extent. The key figure behind the new belief in open water at the poles was August Petermann, who set out to prove his theory in 1869 with two ships, the *Hansa* and the *Germania*.[8] Perhaps the most surprising aspect of Petermann's theory was that many famous scientists in a wide range of fields in the 1860s were convinced he was right, and some even later still.

In France, his admirers included scholars in a number of domains – the geographer Conrad Malte-Brun, the geologist Élie de Beaumont, the meteorologist Edme Hippolyte Marié-Davy, the naturalist Armand de Quatrefages de Bréau, the historian Henri Martin, the science writer Arthur Mangin, author of *Mystères de l'océan* [*Mysteries of the Ocean*, 1864], the geographer Élisée Reclus, Jules Verne, and a number of members of the Institut de France and the French longitude bureau. The 1866 edition of Pierre Larousse's *Dictionnaire universel* [*Universal Dictionary*] informed readers that there was open sea at the poles. That same year, the science writer Charles Grad argued strongly in favour of the theory in the *Comptes rendus de l'Académie des sciences* [*Records of the Academy of Sciences*]. As late as 1873, Jules Gay, a physics teacher at a Montpellier high school, published a school book entitled *La Mer libre du pôle* [*The Open Seas at the Pole*].[9]

The hypothesis of open seas at the poles was based on a series of arguments, three of which were underlined by Élisée Reclus: continuous exposure to the sun for six months, the existence of warm currents, particularly the Gulf Stream, and the belief that the temperature was milder at the poles themselves. Past navigators also claimed to have seen it. These were the points that Jules Michelet drew on in his 1861 book *La Mer*, while Marié-Davy was convinced by the existence of the Gulf Stream.

A secondary argument in favour of open seas at the poles was that many navigators had noticed birds flying north over the pack ice. What would they be going to find if the pole was a place of terrifying cold, devoid of food and nesting opportunities? This case was made by the geographer Charles Hertz. The term 'polynya' – now meaning an expanse of non-frozen water surrounded by sea ice – came into use at mid-century, playing into the theory of a vast open sea at the pole. In the 1860s, the arguments against the theory, claiming that eyewitnesses had been fooled by optical illusions, seemed rather thin. The *Challenger* expedition was particularly significant here. The captain was an ardent proponent of the open sea theory on setting out, but soon changed his mind during the course of the voyage.

One particularly important aspect of the debate from this book's point of view is that almost all the writers who set their novels at the pole – and there were many – described adventurers on a quest to find this fabled open sea. Jules Verne is now by far the most famous. His tremendous novel of 1867, *Les Aventures du capitaine Hatteras*, demonstrates why polar literature was so fashionable for decades and how it convinced readers, quite erroneously, that the mysteries of the poles had been solved:

> 'The sea! the sea!' they all shouted.
>
> 'And the open sea!' cried the captain. [. . .] The ocean stretched beyond the line of vision, with no island or new land peering above the horizon. [. . .] The land of New America thus died away in the Polar Ocean, quietly and gently.

The following chapter, 'The open sea', named the 'polar ocean' by explorers, teems with all sorts of animals and sea monsters in an atmosphere of 'incomparable purity', with great albatrosses wheeling overhead. From time to time, it is struck by storms like cyclones, 'turning rapidly round this peaceful centre'. At one point, Verne writes, 'a whirlpool, a new maelstrom, formed among the waves', dragging down Captain Hatteras.[10]

Expeditions to find open seas at the poles gradually fell out of favour in the 1870s. The concepts of periodical flooding and open seas nonetheless continued to fire the public imagination. We now turn to a brief study of how scientific knowledge about the polar regions was disseminated in accounts of heroic exploits on ship or sledge, combining brave feats of derring-do and scientific discovery.

We have already encountered the greatest French popular science writer of his day, Louis Figuier, who founded the journal *L'Année scientifique* [*The Year in Science*] in 1856. It published the latest polar research. In parallel, mass-market popular science journals showcased Arctic expeditions and polar science, broadly defined, including *L'Illustration* [*Illustration*], *L'Année géographique* [*The Year in Geography*, founded in 1863] and, most significantly, Édouard Charton's *Le Tour du monde* [*World Tour*]. Two even more widely read general interest magazines, *Le Petit journal* and *Le Musée des familles* [*The Family Museum*], described the exploits of the heroic men who set out to conquer the poles, bringing the latest discoveries to a very broad audience indeed.[11]

Even more important, perhaps, were the large numbers of travel narratives and novels featuring the poles. No territory was a greater source of fascination for writers in the latter half of the century, no doubt because it was such an enigma. The former governor of Canada Frederick Hamilton-Temple-Blackwood, 1st Marquess of Dufferin, visited Spitsbergen in 1856, publishing his *Letters from High Latitudes* based on his experiences. The book was translated into French in 1860, inspiring many French writers. Jules Verne set seven of his 'extraordinary adventures' at the poles. Albert Robida's *Les Voyages très extraordinaires de Saturnin Farandoul dans les cinq ou six parties du monde* [*Saturnin Farandoul's Very Extraordinary Adventures in the Five or Six Parts of the World*], including a scene set in the supposedly open seas at the North Pole, enjoyed a wide readership, as did Pierre Maël's *Une Française au pôle Nord* [*A Frenchwoman at the North Pole*, 1893] and Louis-Henri Boussenard's series *L'Enfer des glaces* [*The Icy Hell*, 1893]. The balloonist Édouard Deburaux published *Sur la route du pôle* [*En Route to the Pole*] under the pen name Léo Dex in 1901. This was the last in a long line of polar narratives, far more extensive than this brief list suggests.

These authors fascinated hordes of readers with the gripping adventures of their heroes surviving terrible dangers in the long polar night, from bear attacks and ships trapped in shifting ice to dreadful cold and alluring mirages. Readers were enthralled by the shimmering Northern Lights, heard the creaking of the ice, felt the frostbite in their own fingers, and shivered with dread at the thought of the gnawing hunger that drove men to cannibalism.

Despite the repeated failures of expeditions to the North Pole, late-nineteenth-century scientists were still eager to fill in the gaps in their knowledge of the region. In 1882, meteorologists came together to organize the very first 'international polar year'.

27
The Earth Sciences Slowly Filter into General Knowledge

Writing the history of how science shrank the boundaries of ignorance only makes sense if we consider how such knowledge filtered out from expert circles to the rest of society, via schools, lectures, exhibitions, the media and books. Only when these are taken into account can we arrive at a rough approximation of the social stratification of knowledge.

The third period studied in this book, from 1860 to 1900, corresponds – at least in France – to a golden age of popular science. That is not to say, however, that scientific knowledge was always disseminated effectively.

A thorough study of popular science would involve a number of lists that do not make for interesting reading. The following offers just a brief overview of the situation. In addition to schools, four vectors played a crucial role: the press, various kinds of libraries (and the print material they contained), lectures and exhibitions. The study of the dissemination of knowledge involves the study of reading.

The most effective channel for transmitting scientific thought to a wide audience in the closing decades of the nineteenth century was the scientific journal, ahead of books. At least three categories can be identified.[1] Alongside the proceedings of the major scientific institutions, like France's weekly round-up of events at the Academy of Sciences, a number of field-specific science journals showcased the latest research under the watchful eye of experts. Most of these were produced by laboratories and included bibliographies and reviews of major science publications. They were available in university libraries, laboratories, and leading teaching institutions such as the École normale supérieure and the École pratique des hautes études. This reflected a shift away from the academy model towards the more modern approach to scientific journals which was to dominate the twentieth century.

Daniel Reichvag has recorded some fifty popular science journals published in France from 1850 to 1900.[2] There was also a host of general interest magazines for an educated, intellectually curious but non-expert readership. Their authors saw it as their mission to disseminate learning, devoting many articles, or even entire sections, to science. The late nineteenth century was a golden age for such journals, which often included drawings and even photographs to attract readers. The *Magasin pittoresque*, which began publishing in 1833, called itself a 'popular encyclopedia'. Ten years later, *L'Illustration* began its long life. The year 1850 saw the launch of *Le Tour du monde*, its title a clear indication of its content, followed in 1856 by *L'Année scientifique*. The latter was founded by Édouard Charton and edited by Louis Figuier, one of the century's two great popular science writers in French (the other was Camille Flammarion). Then there were *L'Année géographique*, founded in 1863, and above all Gaston Tissandier's *La Nature* [*Nature*]. Jules Claretie, Albert Robida and Louis Boussenard launched *Le Journal des voyages et des aventures de terre et de mer* [*The Journal of Travels and Adventures by Land and Sea*]: Robida and Boussenard also wrote serial novels of exploration describing what had once been blank spaces on the world map.

The number of specialist and popular science journals rose sharply: in 1800, 750 such journals were published worldwide; by 1885, there were 5,000; by 1895, 80,000. As the century closed, there were an estimated 100,000 science publications annually, including books and journal articles.

The majority of the population did not read such journals, which tended to focus on geography rather than the earth sciences per se. Those living in urban areas could access the *Bibliothèque des merveilles* [*Library of Marvels*] collection and, most importantly, the *Magasin d'éducation et de récréation* [*Magazine for Education and Entertainment*], founded by Jules Hetzel in 1864 to take over from the *Bibliothèque illustrée des familles* [*Illustrated Family Library*]. The *Petite encyclopédie populaire des sciences et de leur applications* [*Little Popular Encyclopedia of the Sciences and their Applications*] is another relevant title.

Alongside these journals, and again largely for an urban readership, came a flood of short handbooks by writers interested in the applied sciences. These humble practitioners of practical science were brilliantly portrayed in Louis-Ferdinand Céline's novel *Mort à crédit* in the figure of Roger-Marin Courtial des Pereires, who was 'a wonder at writing digests, articles, lectures'. His motto was 'spare no effort to enlighten the family and educate the masses'. A portrait of the great Camille Flammarion took pride of place in his applied science journal, *Génitron*, and invoked his name 'like God almighty'. In the course of his career 'he had explained just about everything' and his little handbooks were translated into 'a good many languages [. . .] in a good many schools they were actually a part of the curriculum [. . .] You couldn't imagine anything handier, simpler, easier to assimilate, all predigested!' His classics included a history of polar travel from Maupertuis to Charcot and a family guide to astronomy.[3] Fiction often has much to teach us about the real world!

In rural areas, a greater role was played by gift books and school prizes, often stored away carefully for decades on the top shelf of the wardrobe alongside the household linen. Some such books by specialist publishers such as Ardant in Limoges and Mame in Tours focused on the earth sciences.

All these popular science publications devoted some space to narratives of exploration and adventure. In turn, as we have seen with polar literature, works of fiction drew on cutting-edge scientific research – most notably those of Jules Verne, who owned works by Malte-Brun, Élisée Reclus, Louis Figuier, François Arago and Marié-Davy. His novel *Autour de la Lune* dazzlingly demonstrates how novelists could include the most up-to-date scientific ideas in fiction. Jules Verne, one of the best-selling authors of the century, was a key figure in disseminating modern scientific knowledge to a wide audience.

Another phenomenon typical of the period is the *société savante* or scholarly society, then enjoying something of a golden age in Britain and France. Interestingly, the word 'savant' (scholar) has fallen increasingly out of use in France, from at least the mid-twentieth century, if not earlier. In the latter half of the nineteenth century, it still conferred a degree of social prestige that could be bolstered by membership of several such societies. Joining such institutions doubtless let members slake their *libido sciendi*, but was also a means of increasing their prestige and social capital. In Britain, their members came largely from the middle classes, including newly wealthy manufacturers, merchants, doctors and traders who saw the societies as a means of garnering prestige, setting themselves apart from the landed gentry and above all the unenlightened masses. In France, the local nobility flocked to such societies; for members of the petty and *haute* bourgeoisie, they became a social practice that conferred prestige and recognition at the local level.[4]

What became of the thirst for knowledge in this social context? First and foremost, given that most such societies covered a range of sciences, being a member meant claiming scholarship in several, or even multiple, fields. They also meant that the *libido sciendi* was applied on a small scale, to the local vicinity. The same was true of the approach to science in primary education. Teaching inspectors encouraged French primary school teachers to write books on their local communities; bishops sometimes asked priests to write parish histories. As a result, local scholarly societies tended to focus on areas such as ancient and medieval archaeology, local history, ethnography and botany, studied on organized excursions, as well as regional forms of artistic practice. In this context, the earth sciences were a marginal presence, as indicated by the names of such institutions. Robert Fox has calculated that just five French provincial scholarly societies, or 0.7 per cent of the total, had names referring to meteorology, and four (or 0.6 per cent) to geology or mineralogy.

The main role of these scholarly societies was making science books available to members. There were many types of library at this time. First of all were the municipal libraries in big urban centres, with Paris as a special case. Such libraries built on the holdings of earlier ecclesiastical libraries, gradually adding more recent acquisitions. They were generally only used by scholars, often members of societies. The same was true of the French national library, which opened a public reading room in 1868.

Parish libraries were established by the Œuvre des bons livres [Good Books Charity] to provide suitably devout reading matter for young people and worshippers. Their main holdings were, naturally, improving in nature. Three further types of library made books widely available: station libraries, working men's libraries and school libraries. The first of these offered books to travellers to while away the time. Working men's libraries formed a significant network of institutions with different profiles.[5] The first was founded in 1861 by Jean-Baptiste Girard, a typesetter. The most prestigious was the Bibliothèque des Amis de l'instruction [Library of the Friends of Learning] in Paris's third *arrondissement*, which in 1882 had 360 members and a collection of 5,120 volumes.

Two institutions came to play a key role in the development of working men's libraries. The Franklin Society, founded in Paris in 1862, shared the same ambition as the Amis de l'instruction. The Franklin Society library was open in the evenings and on Sundays. Like most such establishments, it lent books out, so that they could be read by anyone with a job in Paris. The model soon spread to towns across France. By 1900, there were some three thousand such libraries. Neighbouring countries such as Belgium proved just as eager for books: the library network had developed in Britain earlier than France.

The last ten years have seen a number of book-length studies of working men's libraries. Unfortunately, a close reading reveals that the earth sciences did not figure prominently either in their catalogues or among the books borrowed. To take one example, Alan Ritt Baker's study of readers of books broadly classified as 'geography' reveals that such titles were rare in the twenty-two library catalogues surveyed, and even more rarely borrowed. Furthermore, those works that were borrowed were generally travel accounts and narratives of exploration rather than scholarship on the earth sciences proper. The study also covers novels found in working men's libraries, which we will return to later.

A study of library catalogues in the Haute-Vienne *département* of central France for the year 1870 reveals that just 204 titles came under the heading 'sciences and arts'. In the town of Brive in the Corrèze *département*, now renowned for its book fair, just 8.4 per cent of the library's 1,600 books were in the 'science and arts' category, accounting for just 1.6 per cent of loans in 1872.[6]

Perhaps the most important category of libraries, at least in purely numerical terms, were school libraries, established in 1862. The best pupils and the local rural elite could borrow books. An 1877 survey in the Haute-Vienne of reading habits in school libraries, completed by fifty-eight primary school teachers, showed what kinds of books readers (mostly older pupils and young adults) preferred.[7] The survey showed that 1,953 books were borrowed over the course of the year. The biggest categories were agriculture and national history, followed by novels. Just four authors accounted for almost all the novels read. First came Jules Verne, listed fifteen times: *Cinq semaines en ballon* was mentioned eight times as the only book enjoyed by readers. The three others were Captain Mayne Reid, Fenimore Cooper (*The Prairie*, *The Red Rover*, etc.) and Walter Scott (*Quentin Durward* and *Ivanhoe*). These preferences reflect a taste for far-flung adventures rather than the earth sciences. The Haute-Vienne had 333 school libraries in 1877, lending out 10,766 books.

I have not touched on the working men's educational institutes founded in the closing years of the century in Paris, Nancy and Besançon, or the working men's classes and lecture series held mainly in the capital, since these reached a very limited audience.

One channel by which knowledge did reach new audiences was lectures, until at least the mid-twentieth century. Paris hosted well-known series of talks such as the *Annales* lectures, while smaller provincial towns would also organize such events from time to time. Unfortunately for the purposes of this book, such presentations generally focused on accounts of travel and exploration rather than science. The speakers described the flora, fauna and peoples they encountered in remote corners of the earth, sometimes showing photographs and even objects such as animal skins, assegais and talismans. Some popular libraries did occasionally organize lectures on scientific topics: for instance, Camille Flammarion gave a talk in Epernay on 'The earth and the sky, balloon travel, etc.'[8] Missionaries also gave lectures after returning from often relatively short postings abroad to far-flung corners of the planet, and missionary journals were another branch of the press.

One question immediately comes to mind in terms of reducing ignorance of the earth's mysteries in the decades between 1860 and 1900. What role did schools play? This was a time when literacy was gaining ground fast and pupils now had schoolbooks, particularly for geography, which became a compulsory subject in 1867. It is fair to say that the curriculum did not reflect much of the research covered in this book. Knowledge of the earth, particularly its most terrifying aspects, was generally limited to its shape, the flattening at the poles, and sometimes its ecliptic tilt. The earth's crust was often compared in appearance to a baked apple.

At the same time, the school curriculum began to focus, at least in France, on local regions, seen as 'little homelands';[9] schoolmasters and learned societies wrote books on their local areas and took their pupils out on walks, as promoted by the geographer Élisée Reclus, to teach them to read the local landscape.

I have discussed how people learned to study the lie of the land around them thanks to advances in geology, developing a feel for the morphology of river basins and courses. Schoolchildren were encouraged to develop this sense for themselves on walks, giving them the love of learning that Élisée Reclus considered so important. He held that 'the first period of civilization was coming to an end' – the 'period of primitive ignorance' – and that it was too late to eschew the benefits of science in the hope of 'rediscovering joy in the simplicity of ignorance'.

Reclus had a very clear vision of how geography should be taught.[10] He gave pride of place to studying the nature of the earth by means of 'direct observation of the Earth that saw our birth'. The best way to achieve this, he wrote, was by walks 'around the customary place of residence' and 'conversations arising from the view of objects and landscapes', which

> would be different in a land of plains and a land of mountains, in granite regions and limestone regions, by the ocean, by a major river, or heathlands [. . .] we would observe everywhere a certain diversity of terrains, with sand, clay, swamp, peat, and probably also sandstone and limestone; everywhere we could follow the bank of a stream or river, watch a current flow, an eddy swirl, an ebb sweeping water upstream, the play of wrinkles on the sand, the progress of erosion along the bank and the alluvions settling on

> sand bars. The opportunity to see showers [. . .] and the sky. [. . .] We see fogs, clouds covering the blue sky, then the great, rare spectacles of the storm, lightning, rainbows, maybe even the Northern Lights.

Only then, Reclus believed, would geography lessons come alive, helping children to read the atlases and globes in their classrooms. Reclus was keen to help children understand the natural world around them geologically, geographically and meteorologically, echoing the message of the Vidal de La Blache school of thought and making the local region the focal point of primary teaching.

Peter Kropotkin shared many of Reclus's thoughts, in educational theory and politics alike: both were early anarchists. Kropotkin wrote a lengthy work in praise of geography as a ferment for the imagination and outlining how it should be taught across the board, to children of obligatory school age up to university students: 'First of all [. . .] the study of the laws to which the modifications of the earth's crust are subjected; the laws [. . .] determining the growth and disappearance of continents, their arrangements past and present, the direction of certain cataclysms [. . .] all subjected to certain telluric laws'. Kropotkin mentions 'tectonic uplifts' and the series of 'geological era'.

He also wrote that some laws of the earth's crust remained to be discovered: 'the orography of the four great continents is as yet at an embryonic stage'. He pleaded for a rapprochement between geology and geography, wishing for 'geographers at great ease in geology'. On teaching younger children, he wrote, 'Even small inequalities in the height of the ground can give a child an idea of what a mountain, a high plateau, a summit, or glacier is, and only on a map of his own village or town can he grasp the conventional hieroglyphs on our maps.'

The writings of Élisée Reclus and Peter Kropotkin on how to teach the data covered in this book might seem idealistic. Yet the French earth sciences curriculum was indeed shaped by their ideas and what they hoped to see, until at least the mid-twentieth century. Class walks – with or without teachers – and a focus on the local region, including the natural region for older children, as well as geology, hydrology, fluvialism and the geological landscape dominated the teaching of geography all the way through to university level in the mid-twentieth century. When I was studying for the postgraduate *agrégation* examination, I remember studying hydrology, reading big books on each of France's 'natural regions', and spending hours drawing and commenting on geological cross-sections with the help of specialist maps. The curriculum still reflected centres of interest that arose in the latter half of the nineteenth century, studied in this chapter.

Some readers might be surprised that I have not mentioned exhibitions, displays and museums devoted to far-flung corners of the earth. I have deliberately not included them because in general, their aim was to showcase the lives of indigenous peoples and villages across the planet. They do not represent one of the forms of ignorance that this book has sought to record. They featured tens of thousands of photographs of bodies, saved from oblivion and read in terms of the dominant racialist theories of the nineteenth century.

Some aspects of the nineteenth century's world fairs were, however, relevant. The universal exhibition held in Paris in 1900 is an exceptional source, not for its indigenous villages – a topic that has been widely researched – but for the large-scale installations that sought to demonstrate the earth's place in the cosmos as accurately as possible.[11]

Two such installations were seen by tens of thousands of visitors. The first was the siderostat, a great mirror moved by clockwork to follow a patch of sky, at the Palais de l'optique [Palace of Optics] at the foot of the Eiffel Tower; the second was Albert Galeron's Cosmorama, or 'Galeron sphere', on avenue de Solférino, outside the exhibition proper but still connected to it. Such installations were influential because they attempted to simulate the planet itself, as dioramas had done in the early years of the century, but on a far grander scale.

The Palais de l'optique also contained a number of 'secondary attractions' presented by Fortuné Méaulle – images that took visitors into the earth's deep history, its 'first crust', 'great rainfalls', 'beginnings of the sea', 'coal forests', 'reptiles in the Triassic period' and 'fighting dinosaurs'. Louis Rousselet wrote a work in 1901 describing the exhibition. Among the subjects on display at the Palais de l'optique he listed pictures of 'the seabed' and 'subterranean landscapes', which can only have been imaginary, given that the great depths beneath the earth's crust were still unknown. It also featured bird's-eye views of the earth taken from a balloon. All these depictions must have made a particular impression on visitors thanks to the use of stereoscopy, then becoming commonplace.

Albert Galeron's Cosmorama depicted the earth at the centre of a model of the solar system some sixty metres in height. The earth lay in a dish of mercury, spinning slowly on its axis. There was room for one hundred visitors at a time to peer down at the display through portholes placed at different heights around the outer shell.

Both the Palais de l'optique and the Cosmorama

aimed to stir a range of emotions in visitors discovering the planet earth, its deep past and its place in the cosmos. From the perspective of this book, such spectacular means of disseminating information on the earth sciences were significant, but perhaps not the most important vector.

The images of the moon captured by the siderostat's great mirror generated emotions even more intense than the photographs then found in books. The apparatus meant visitors could study the moon's surface in great detail and picture themselves as aliens treading its surface. Extremely detailed photographs of the moon and its craters were likewise on display. Defining the moon's craters caused a debate. Most people compared them visually to volcanic craters on earth, which seemed the obvious solution. However, some scientists argued against this interpretation, since there were no cones at the base of the craters, which meant they could not share the same cause as volcanoes on earth.

Variations in the moon's shape and light and lunar eclipses had always been known, while its influence on the tides was a more recent discovery. More fine-grained knowledge of its morphology, including the undeniable existence of craters, meant it began to be seen as a kind of second earth. This is a fine place to close our investigation. Ignorance about the moon was shrinking, while ignorance of the earth remained more widespread than historians often implicitly suggest.

28

Measuring Ignorance at the Dawn of the Twentieth Century

At the dawn of the twentieth century, much still remained unknown about the earth, though giant steps had been taken since 1860 – far more rapidly than in the eighteenth century. The closing pages of this book will attempt to justify the considerable anxiety, even terror, that ignorance still inspired, quite understandably.

In 1900, the poles were still an enigma. They were places of tragedy, the greatest and most mysterious of all the blank spaces left on the map. By this date, men had mapped the geography of the seabed and dredged up brand-new species of flora and fauna. But no one had physically explored the depths of the oceans; diving suits remained largely in the realms of fantasy.

The depths of the earth's crust beyond the reach of miners likewise remained a mystery, as did the highest altitudes before the troposphere and stratosphere were defined in 1902; they still lay beyond the reach of manned flight. Volcanoes were thought to spew lava from the earth's fiery interior, but the issue was still open to debate – though Krakatoa had clearly demonstrated the effects of eruptions and how they were propagated. The planet was known to have fault lines, though they had not yet been explicitly linked with earthquakes, whose scale was beginning to be measured scientifically. Dynamic meteorology, identifying the circulation of masses of air, cyclones, anticyclones and depressions, was still in its infancy, making weather forecasting an inexact science.

Ignorance of the earth, once total, had indeed shrunk considerably in the course of forty years. The planet's estimated age was somewhat closer to what we now know to be the case today. The mechanisms by which geological strata are laid down, uplifted, fractured and folded back were now clearly understood, as were the effects of the many forms of erosion. The way glaciers eroded valleys, shaped plains and carved the surface of the earth during the multiple Quaternary glacial periods was well known. Hydrologists were beginning to understand how water circulated underground, and the sources of the world's great rivers had been located. The most important change was doubtless the way that people now looked at the earth as a result of this newfound knowledge.

News now went round the world in a flash. But though men and goods were certainly also travelling faster, it is important not to overstate the case. Aeroplanes had not yet taken to the skies, cars were a brand-new invention, and motorcycles made their appearance at the very end of the nineteenth century. From 1755 to 1900, the top speed of transport more or less doubled, from 60 kilometres an hour on a horse at full gallop to 130 kilometres an hour in a car. The great railway revolution symbolized this acceleration since the 1830s. Steam liners criss-crossed the seas, causing much wonderment in their contemporaries, but they were not fast and sail power was still in widespread use.

The data driving the reduction of ignorance was

now more widely accessible than before. But again, it is important not to overstate the case. Schools, with their gaze firmly focused on their local region, and the press, more interested in exploration, new flora and fauna, and ethnography, did not entirely reshape what the population at large knew about the planet earth. That was not their aim.

The forms of knowledge that might have made the world a less mysterious and terrifying place remained relatively inaccessible to non-specialist audiences in the latter half of the nineteenth century. The great scientific institutions and academies published journals and proceedings, read by specialists and a few cultivated amateurs. Popular science journals and writers like Louis Figuier and Camille Flammarion in France also helped shrink the boundaries of ignorance, mainly in urban areas both large and small.

Libraries of all shapes and sizes, run by schools, working men's clubs, parishes and town councils, offered little in the way of reading on the earth sciences, and what little there was rarely attracted readers. The only truly successful and effective vector for widening access to scientific knowledge in libraries, attracting readers in abundance, was contemporary novels by the likes of Jules Verne, Captain Mayne Reid and Xavier Marmier. Jules Verne in particular played a crucial role in raising awareness of scientific debates in all the areas explored in this book. Xavier Marmier's polar literature reflected the great interest of the day in the far north of our planet.

As young men, John Ruskin, Émile Zola, Leo Tolstoy and Marcel Proust had known far more about their planet than Voltaire, Rousseau, Chateaubriand and even Goethe had when the century opened. Yet there was still much they did not know. Across the population as a whole, very few people knew more than the rest of their community. Only later did knowledge become swiftly stratified – a process that is still ongoing.

By around 1880, the world was more or less mapped out. It might have been expected that this might prompt mass enthusiasm for the earth sciences per se, but this was not really the case.

Today – focusing on the field of research covered in this book – knowledge is fast becoming highly stratified. The combined advances of computing, nanotechnologies, artificial intelligence and robotics are truly head-spinning. The study of the cosmos, dark matter, the billions of galaxies, black holes, the structure of the sun and many other topics raises profound questions about the planet earth and its future.

The species *Homo sapiens* is now known to have existed for far longer than was believed just a few decades ago. Satellite archaeology has shed startling new light on the past. It has recently been discovered that a number of small mammal species lived alongside the dinosaurs, ready to take over the world when the dinosaurs died out. These few examples, chosen from among countless others, give the measure of our vast ignorance about our planet's place in the cosmos, the threats facing it, and the age of the species inhabiting it – including us.

Such considerations have broader social relevance. For some thirty years now, knowledge has become stratified at a much more dizzying pace, which inevitably impacts human relationships. The diversity of knowledge makes it difficult for people to communicate – a situation that might seem paradoxical in an age of instant messaging and social networks. This diversity seems likely to be one factor in the decline of Paris's bistro culture and the cafés and taverns that were once the great hubs of village and rural life. For people to engage in enjoyable, spontaneous conversation, they must know that they share more or less the same ground in terms of what they do and do not know. Otherwise, people stick to their own bubbles.

This social impact makes measuring ignorance an important duty for historians. Knowing and understanding our forebears means taking the measure of what they did *not* know. This approach to history sheds light on their decisions and thought patterns. That is why I wrote this book as a plea for a history of ignorance.

Notes

A Comprehensive History Implies the Study of Ignorance

1 Jacques-Henri Bernardin de Saint-Pierre, *The Works of Saint-Pierre: Comprising His Studies of Nature, Paul and Virginia and Indian Cottage: With a Memoir of the Author and Explanatory Notes*, vol. 2, tr. E. Clarke. London: Henry Bohn, 1846, pp. 408–9.
2 Ibid., p. 406.

1 The Great Lisbon Earthquake of 1755

1 These opening paragraphs were inspired by Thomas Labbé's recent major work of scholarship, *Les Catastrophes naturelles au Moyen Âge*. Paris: CNRS, 2017, pp. 185, 188.
2 Petrarch, *Letters on Familiar Matters*, vol. 1, tr. Aldo S. Bernardo. New York: Italica, 2005, p. 245.
3 Jean Delumeau, *La Peur en Occident, XIVe–XVIIIe siècle: Une cité assiégée*. Paris: Fayard, 1978.
4 Labbé, *Les Catastrophes naturelles*, pp. 294–5.
5 The importance of signs of catastrophe is highlighted by Thomas Labbé and by Philippe Bénéton, whose study of Niccolò Massimo (*Niccolò Massimo: Essai*

sur l'art d'écrire de Machiavel. Paris: Cerf, 2018) focuses at length on the importance of disasters as signs in Machiavelli's Florence (ibid., pp. 66–7), quoting a chapter from his *Florentine Histories* (VI-34) mentioning a terrifying tornado in 1456.

6 Henri Brémond, *Histoire littéraire du sentiment religieux en France [1916–1932]*. Paris: Armand Colin, 1969. We will return to natural theology throughout the present book.

7 Translator's note: the word 'catastrophe' had been used in the modern sense in English since the 1530s.

8 The following pages draw on two books crucial to our understanding of the disaster: Grégory Quenet, *Les Tremblements de terre aux XVIIe et XVIIIe siècles: La naissance d'un risque*. Seyssel: Champ Vallon, 2005; and Anne-Marie Mercier-Faivre and Chantal Thomas (eds.), *L'Invention de la catastrophe au XVIIIe siècle: Du châtiment divin au désastre naturel*. Geneva: Droz, 2008.

9 Mercier-Faivre and Thomas, *L'Invention de la catastrophe au XVIIIe siècle*, p. 8.

10 Quenet, *Les Tremblements de terre aux XVIIe et XVIIIe siècles*, p. 358.

11 On how information about the disaster spread, see Anna Saada, 'Le désir d'informer: le tremblement de terre de Lisbonne', in Mercier-Faivre and Thomas, *L'Invention de la catastrophe au XVIIIe siècle*, pp. 209–30.

12 Quenet, *Les Tremblements de terre aux XVIIe et XVIIIe siècles*, p. 367.

13 Muriel Brot, 'La vision matérialiste de Diderot', in Mercier-Faivre and Thomas, *L'Invention de la catastrophe au XVIIIe siècle*, pp. 75–91.

14 Quenet, *Les Tremblements de terre aux XVIIe et XVIIIe siècles*, p. 348.

2 The Age of the Earth?

1 Alain Corbin, *Le Territoire du vide: L'Occident et le désir de rivage (1750–1840)*. Paris: Aubier, 1988; English translation *The Lure of the Sea: The Discovery of the Seaside in the Western World, 1750–1840*, tr. Jocelyn Phelps. Cambridge: Polity, 1994.

2 Jacques-Bénigne Bossuet, *Œuvres*. Paris: Gallimard, 1961, p. 1472.

3 Jacques-Bénigne Bossuet, *A Universal History from the Beginning of the World to the Empire of Charlemagne*, tr. James Elphinston. London: David Steel, 1767, p. 11.

4 Jean de La Bruyère, *Characters*, tr. N. Rowe. London: D. Browne, 1752, pp. 188–9.

5 Georges-Louis Leclerc, Comte de Buffon, 'Des époques de la nature', in *Œuvres*. Paris: Gallimard, 2007, pp. 1193–1342.

6 There is some evidence for this argument as early as Buffon's 1749 work *Théorie de la Terre* [*Theory of the Earth*].

7 Osmo Pekonen and Anouchka Vasak, *Maupertuis en Laponie: À la recherche de la figure de la Terre*. Paris: Hermann, 2014.

8 Jacques-Henri Bernardin de Saint-Pierre, *Studies of Nature*, tr. Henry Hunter. Philadelphia: Joseph Woodward, 1835, p. 67.

9 Ibid., p. 69. Translation modified.

3 Imagining Earth's Internal Structure

1 Vincent Deparis and Hilaire Legros, *Voyage à l'intérieur de la Terre: De la géographie antique à la géophysique moderne: Une histoire des idées*. Paris: CNRS, 2002, p. 18. The following pages owe much to this remarkable book.

2 Ibid., p. 142.
3 Ibid., p. 113ff.
4 Quoted in ibid., pp. 198–9.
5 Georges-Louis Leclerc, Comte de Buffon, *Buffon's Natural History, Containing A Theory of the Earth*, tr. James Smith Barr. London: Printed for the proprietor, 1797, p. 7.
6 Deparis and Legros, *Voyage à l'intérieur de la Terre*, pp. 232–3.
7 Ibid., p. 233.
8 Ibid.

4 The Mystery of the Poles

1 Frédérique Rémy, *Histoire des pôles: Mythes et réalités polaires, 17e–18e siècles*. Paris: Desjonquères, 2009, p. 31. The following pages draw on this excellent book.
2 Quoted in Muriel Brot, 'À la recherche des passages du Nord-Est et du Nord-Ouest: Le regard des navigateurs sur l'Arctique, de Wilhem Barentsz à James Cook', in Jacques Berchtold, Emmanuel Le Roy Ladurie, Jean-Paul Sermain and Anouchka Vasak (eds.), *Canicules et froids extrêmes*. Paris: Hermann, 2012, p. 75. See also Muriel Brot, *Destination Arctique: Sur la représentation des glaces polaires du XVIe au XIXe siècle*. Paris: Hermann, 2015.
3 Ibid., p. 90.
4 Rémy, *Histoire des pôles*, p. 11.
5 Ibid., p. 12.
6 This passage draws on ibid., pp. 39–43.
7 Ibid., p. 92.

5 The Unfathomable Mysteries of the Deep

1 Jean-René Vanney, *Le Mystère des abysses: Histoire et découvertes des profondeurs océaniques*. Paris:

Fayard, 1993, p. 74. This admirable book by a leading specialist could be quoted here at considerable length.

2 Ibid., p. 12.
3 Ibid., pp. 75, 76.
4 Ibid., p. 76.
5 See Alain Corbin and Hélène Richard (eds.), *La Mer: Terreur et fascination*. Paris: BnF/Seuil, 2004.
6 Vanney, *Le Mystère des abysses*, p. 133. See also Margaret Deacon's seminal work of scholarship, *Scientists and the Sea, 1650–1900: A Study of Marine Science*. London/New York: Academic Press, 1971, which I drew on heavily for ch. 1 of my earlier work *The Lure of the Sea*.
7 Vanney, *Le Mystère des abysses*, p. 123.
8 Ibid.
9 Ibid., p. 125.
10 Corbin, *Lure of the Sea*, p. 109.
11 Vanney, *Le Mystère des abysses*, p. 142; and Benoît de Maillet, *Telliamed ou Entretien d'un philosophe indien avec un missionnaire français*. Amsterdam: Printed by the author, 1748.

6 Discovering Mountains

1 Serge Briffaud, *Naissance d'un paysage: La montagne pyrénéenne à la croisée des regards (XVIe–XIXe siècle)*. Toulouse: Archives des Hautes Pyrénées/CIMA-CNRS-Université de Toulouse-Le Mirail, 1994, pref. Alain Corbin. The following paragraphs draw on this fine book.
2 Ibid., esp. p. 171.
3 Claude Reichler, *La Découverte des Alpes et la question du paysage*. Geneva: Georg, 2002, p. 35.
4 François Dagognet, *Essai philosophique sur la thérapeutique médicale: L'évolution des idées sur*

l'oxygène et la cure d'air. Unpublished PhD thesis, Université de Lyon, 1958.

5 Horace Bénédict de Saussure, *Voyages dans les Alpes*. Geneva: Georg, 2002, p. 171.

6 Ibid.

7 Reichler, *La Découverte des Alpes et la question du paysage*, p. 69.

8 Philippe Joutard, *L'Invention du mont Blanc*. Paris: Gallimard, 1986.

9 Saussure, *Voyages dans les Alpes*, p. 194.

10 The cognitive richness of mountains will be a recurrent theme in later chapters on storms, cave systems and glaciers.

11 See David McCallam, 'Face à la mort blanche: conceptions du froid extrême dans les avalanches et dans les neiges au XVIIIe siècle', in Berchtold et al., *Canicules et froids extrêmes*, pp. 97–108.

7 Mysterious Glaciers

1 Frédérique Rémy, *Histoire de la glaciologie*. Paris: Vuibert, 2008, p. 8.

2 Reichler, *La Découverte des Alpes et la question du paysage*, pp. 122–3.

3 Rémy, *Histoire de la glaciologie*, p. 73.

4 Ibid., p. 77.

5 Reichler, *La Découverte des Alpes et la question du paysage*, p. 35.

6 Ibid.

8 A Fascination with Volcanoes

1 Quenet, *Les Tremblements de terre au XVIIe et XVIIIe siècles*, p. 469.

2 Alexander von Humboldt, *Cosmos: A Sketch of a Physical Description of the Universe*, vol. 1, tr. E. Otté. London: Henry Bohn, 1849, p. 227.

3 Dominique Bertrand (ed.), *L'Invention du paysage volcanique*. Clermont-Ferrand: Presses universitaires Blaise-Pascal, 2004. The following paragraphs draw on this essential work of scholarship. See also Antonella Tufano, *Les Paysages volcaniques: Les mythes, la science, l'art*. Paris: EHESS, 2000.

4 Dominique Bertrand, 'Décrire l'Etna à la Renaissance: entre mémoire culturelle et autopsie', in *L'Invention du paysage volcanique*, pp. 39–46.

5 On William Hamilton, see Jean Arrouye, 'Le paysage volcanique scientifique dans les *Campi Phlegræi* de William Hamilton', in Bertrand, *L'Invention du paysage volcanique*, pp. 71–82.

6 See Friedrich Wolfzettel, 'Flora Tristan et les volcans sublimes', in Bertrand, *L'Invention du paysage volcanique*, p. 113ff.

7 Ibid.

8 See Alexis Drahos, *Orages et tempêtes, volcans et glaciers: Les peintres et les sciences de la Terre au XVIIIe siècle*. Paris: Hazan, 2014.

9 Quoted in ibid., p. 67.

10 Geneviève Goubier-Robert, 'De la fulguration sadienne aux foudres républicaines', in Berchtold et al., *Canicules et froids extrêmes*, p. 430.

11 On the series of volcanic eruptions, see Richard Hamblyn, *The Invention of Clouds: How an Amateur Meteorologist Forged the Language of the Skies*. London: Picador, 2001, pp. 55–6.

12 Quoted in David McCallam, 'Un météore inédit: les brouillards secs de 1783', in Thierry Belleguic and Anouchka Vasak (eds.), *Ordre et désordre du monde*. Paris: Hermann, 2013. For all the data quoted below, see ibid., pp. 369–86.

9 The Birth of Meteorology

1 Hamblyn, *Invention of Clouds*, p. 97.
2 Olivier Jandot, *Les Délices du feu: L'homme, le chaud et le froid à l'époque moderne*. Ceyzérieu: Champ Vallon, 2017.
3 William Shakespeare, *Antony and Cleopatra*. London: Penguin, 2007.
4 Quoted in Hamblyn, *Invention of Clouds*, p. 91.
5 Karine Becker, '"[. . .] leur prêter des traits, un corps, une âme, un nom" (Lamartine)', in Pierre Glaudes and Anouchka Vasak (eds.), *Les Nuages: Du tournant des Lumières au crépuscule du romantisme (1760–1880)*. Paris: Hermann, 2017, p. 215.
6 See Jean Vassord, *Les Papiers d'un laboureur au Siècle des lumières: Pierre Bordier: Une culture paysanne*. Ceyzérieu: Champ Vallon, 1999.
7 Alain Corbin, *Histoire de la pluie*. Paris: Flammarion, 2017; Corbin, *Village Bells: Sound and Meaning in the Nineteenth-Century French Countryside*, tr. M. Thom. New York: Columbia University Press, 1998.
8 Muriel Collart, 'La fabrique des nuages: Une simulation expérimentale au XVIIIe siècle', in Glaudes and Vasak, *Les Nuages*, p. 85.
9 Jacques-Henri Bernardin de Saint-Pierre, *Études de la nature*. Saint-Étienne: Publications de l'université de Saint-Étienne, 2007, p. 465.
10 Saussure, *Voyage dans les Alpes*, pp. 237–8.
11 Anouchka Vasak, *Météorologies: Discours sur le ciel et le climat des Lumières au romantisme*. Paris: Honoré Champion, 2007, p. 78, quoted in her remarkable chapter on the storm of 13 July 1788.

12 Understanding Glaciers

1 See Rémy, *Histoire de la glaciologie*; Rémy, *Le Monde givré*. Paris: Hermann, 2016; and Marc-Antoine Kaeser, *Un savant séducteur: Louis Agassiz (1807–1873), prophète de la science*. Neuchâtel: Éditions de l'Aire, 2007.
2 Kaeser, *Un savant séducteur*, p. 106.
3 Rémy, *Histoire de la glaciologie*, p. 80.
4 Kaeser, *Un savant séducteur*, p. 112.

13 The Birth of Geology

1 In 1830, geology and physical geography were two very distinct fields. This duality shaped, and often muddied, scientific research in both in the West.
2 Jean-Pierre Chaline, *Sociabilité et érudition: Les sociétés savantes en France, XIXe–XXe siècles*. Paris: CTHS, 1998; and Odile Parsis-Barubé, *La Province antiquaire: L'invention de l'histoire locale en France (1800–1870)*. Paris: CTHS, 2011.
3 Corbin, *Le Territoire du vide*.
4 Deparis and Legros, *Voyage à l'intérieur de la Terre*, p. 300.
5 Gustave Flaubert, *Bouvard and Pécuchet*, tr. A. J. Krailsheimer. London: Penguin, 1976. See also Jean Goguel (ed.), *La Terre*. Paris: Gallimard, 1959. It should be borne in mind that the history of what our forebears did *not* know is vital in avoiding psychological anachronism.

14 Volcanoes and the Mystery of 'Dry Fogs'

1 The first major piece of scholarship on this subject was Richard B. Stothers, 'The great Tambora eruption and its aftermath', *Science*, 15 June 1984, pp. 1191–7. The best recent work on the topic is Gillen d'Arcy Wood, *Tambora: The Eruption that*

Changed the World. Princeton/Oxford: Princeton University Press, 2014. The following paragraphs draw on this account.
2 Ibid., p. 69.
3 Wolfgang Behringer, *Tambora und das Jahr ohne Sommer: Wie ein Vulkan die Welt in die Krise stürzte*. Munich: Beck, 2015. Interestingly, the first crisis coincided with the Congress of Vienna.
4 On artists and writers, see Anouchka Vasak, '1816, l'année sans été', in David Spurr and Nicolas Ducimetière (eds.), *Frankenstein créé des ténèbres*. Paris: Fondation Martin Bodmer/Gallimard, 2016.
5 D'Arcy Wood, *Tambora*, p. 51.
6 For the following paragraphs, see ibid.
7 Ibid.

15 The Ocean Depths and Fear of the Unknown
1 Vanney, *Le Mystère des abysses*, p. 141.
2 Ibid., p. 142.
3 Ibid., p. 149.
4 On the preceding paragraphs, see ibid., pp. 151–3.
5 Ibid., p. 163.

16 Reading Clouds and the Beaufort Scale
1 Hamblyn, *Invention of Clouds*.
2 On Howard's nomenclature, see Anouchka Vasak, 'L'invention des nuages (Luke Howard, 1803)', in Glaudes and Vasak, *Les Nuages*, pp. 154–63.
3 Quoted in Hamblyn, *Invention of Clouds*, pp. 120, 123.
4 Johann Wolfgang von Goethe, 'Wolkengestalt nach Howard', in *Sämtliche Werke, Briefe, Tagebücher und Gespräche*, vol. 25, ed. W. Engelhardt and M. Menzel. Frankfurt am Main: Frankfurter Ausgabe, 1989, pp. 214–44.

5 Fabien Locher, *Le Savant et la tempête: Étudier l'atmosphère et prévoir le temps au XIXe siècle*. Rennes: PUR, 2008.
6 Victor Hugo, *La Mer et le Vent*, quoted by Françoise Chenet, 'Hugo ou l'art de déconcerter les anémomètres', in Michel Viegnes (ed.), *Imaginaires du vent*. Paris: Imago, 2003, pp. 304–5.
7 Alexander Dalrymple devised his own scale at around the same time, but it failed to gain traction. On the Beaufort scale, see Hamblyn, *Invention of Clouds*, pp. 200–1.
8 See Locher, *Le Savant et la tempête*, p. 14ff.
9 For a rich anthology of these texts, see Raphaël Troubac, *Le Théâtre que des hommes voyaient pour la première fois: Les impressions physiques et morales des premiers hommes à avoir atteint de hautes altitudes en ballon (1783–1850)*. Unpublished MA dissertation supervised by Alain Corbin, université Paris I-Panthéon-Sorbonne, 1999.

17 The Poles Remain a Mystery

1 These paragraphs draw on Bertrand Imbert and Claude Lorius, *Le Grand défi des pôles*. Paris: Gallimard, 2006; and Rémy, *Histoire des pôles*.
2 Canadian researchers found the wreck of the *Erebus* in 2014 and 2015, aided by Inuit traditions and the discovery of instruments along the coastline. This wrote a new chapter in the history of the disaster, proving that the *Erebus* eventually put back to sea with several sailors who did not abandon ship with the rest of the crew.
3 D'Arcy Wood, *Tambora*, pp. 147–8.

19 Exploring the Ocean Depths

1 One of my own great-uncles was a transatlantic cable winchman at the turn of the twentieth century; I remember he had to move around a lot for his work.

2 Numa Broc, *Une histoire de la géographie physique*. Perpignan: Presses universitaires de Perpignan, 2010, vol. I, p. 196.

3 Ibid.

4 Vanney, *Le Mystère des abysses*, p. 229.

5 Quoted in ibid.

6 Ibid., p. 252.

20 The Development of Dynamic Meteorology

1 Joëlle Dusseau, *Jules Verne et la mer*, forthcoming.

2 Alain Corbin, 'Le paquebot ou la vacuité de l'espace et du temps', in Alain Corbin (ed.), *L'Avènement des loisirs*. Paris: Aubier, 1995, pp. 62–80.

3 On the preceding paragraphs, see Locher, *Le Savant et la tempête*.

4 On the preceding paragraphs, see Broc, *Une histoire de la géographie physique*, vol. I, p. 359ff.

5 On the quarrel between Mathieu de la Drôme and Urbain Le Verrier, see Locher, *Le Savant et la tempête*, pp. 83–104.

21 Manned Flight and the Discovery of the Troposphere and Stratosphere

1 For these paragraphs, see Fabien Locher, 'Explorer l'atmosphère', in *Le Savant et la tempête*, pp. 176–188.

2 Camille Flammarion, quoted in ibid., p. 175.

3 See Broc, *Une histoire de la géographie physique*, vol. I, pp. 191–2.

22 Scientific Volcanology and the Birth of Seismology

1 Bertrand, *L'Invention du paysage volcanique*, p. 8.

2 See Thanh-Vân Ton-That, 'Entre géographie et poésie: les paysages volcaniques d'Élisée Reclus', in Bertrand, *L'Invention du paysage volcanique*, pp. 109–10.

3 On the preceding paragraphs, see Broc, *Une histoire de la géographie physique*, vol. I, pp. 138–9.

4 Patrick Boucheron, 'Le Krakatoa', in Pierre Singaravélou and Sylvain Venayre (eds.), *Histoire du monde au XIXe siècle*. Paris: Fayard, 2017, pp. 331–6.

5 On these scientific theories, see Broc, *Une histoire de la géographie physique*, vol. I, pp. 141–4.

23 Measuring the Grip of Ice

1 See ibid., pp. 127–8, 130–1.

2 Ibid., p. 131.

3 Ibid.

4 Joseph Fournier identified the greenhouse effect as early as 1824.

5 Frédéric Zurcher and Élie Margollé, *Les Glaciers*, wood engravings by L. Sabatier. Paris: Hachette, 1868.

6 On the club's history, see André Rauch, 'Naissance du Club alpin français: la convivialité, la nature et l'État (1874–1880)', in Pierre Arnaud (ed.), *La Naissance du mouvement sportif associatif. 1879–1914*. Lyon: Presses universitaires de Lyon, 1986, pp. 275–85.

24 Solving the Mysteries of Rivers: Fluvialism, Hydrology and Speleology

1 The study of rivers and their effects.

2 Victor Hugo, *Le Rhin*, in *Oeuvres complètes: Voyages*. Paris: Robert Laffont, 1987, pp. 97–9.
3 Ibid., p. 100.
4 Ibid., p. 119.
5 Ibid., p. 232.
6 Ibid., p. 234.
7 Ibid., pp. 252, 253.
8 Élisée Reclus, 'Le Mississipi: études et souvenirs', *Revue des Deux Mondes*, 15 July and 1 August 1859, quoted by Broc, *Une histoire de la géographie physique*, vol. I, p. 169.
9 Élisée Reclus, 'Le bassin des Amazones et les Indiens', *Revue des Deux Mondes*, 15 June 1862, quoted by Broc, *Une histoire de la géographie physique*, vol. I, p. 170.
10 Élisée Reclus, *Histoire d'un ruisseau*. Arles: Actes Sud, 2005.
11 Broc, *Une histoire de la géographie physique*, vol. I, p. 160.
12 The agreement was reached at a conference in Bern on the problem of river sources. See ibid., p. 170.

25 A New Approach to Reading the Globe

1 Another debate that captivated geologists from the 1860s on was whether the earth could change shape. Was the planet's shape fixed, or might it adapt to prevailing forces by means of viscosity or elasticity? The debate did not extend beyond highly specialized circles and is therefore not immediately relevant for this chapter. See Deparis and Legros, *Voyage à l'intérieur de la Terre*; and Broc, *Une histoire de la géographie physique*.
2 Conrad Malte-Brun, *Précis de géographie universelle ou Description de toutes les parties du monde*. Paris: F. Buisson, 1810–29.

3 The branch of geology dealing with the formation, evolution, localization and composition of the mineral masses comprising the globe.
4 Quoted in Broc, *Une histoire de la géographie physique*, vol. I, p. 104.
5 See the previous chapter.

26 Was There Open Sea at the Poles?

1 Chantal Edel, 'La course aux pôles', *Reliefs*, 3, 2016, p. 34.
2 On all these expeditions, see Rémy, *Histoire des pôles*; and Imbert and Lorius, *Le Grand défi des pôles*.
3 The North-West Passage was eventually discovered in 1905 by Roald Amundsen, who set sail from Oslo in 1903.
4 See Rémy, *Le Monde givré*, p. 82ff.
5 Ibid., p. 173.
6 Ibid., p. 151.
7 Ibid., pp. 96–7.
8 Ibid., pp. 106–9.
9 Ibid., p. 124.
10 Jules Verne, *The Voyages and Adventures of Captain Hatteras*. Boston: James R. Osgood, 1876.
11 See ibid., p. 145ff.

27 The Earth Sciences Slowly Filter into General Knowledge

1 The following draws on Vincent Duclert and Anne Rasmussen's seminal article 'Les revues scientifiques et la dynamique de la recherche', in Jacqueline Pluet-Despatin, Michel Leymarie and Jean-Yves Mollier (eds.), *La Belle époque des revues (1880–1914)*. Saint-Germain-la-Blanche-Herbe: Éditions de l'IMEC, 2002, pp. 237–55. See also Bernadette

Bensaude-Vincent and Anne Rasmussen (eds.), *La Science populaire dans la presse et l'édition (XIXe–XXe siècles)*. Paris: CNRS, 1997.

2 Daniel Reichvag and Jean Jacques, *Savants et ignorants: Une histoire de la vulgarisation des sciences*. Paris: Seuil, 1991.

3 Louis-Ferdinand Céline, *Death on Credit*, tr. R. Manheim. Richmond: Alma, 2009, p. 283.

4 See Jean-Pierre Chaline, Robert Fox and George Weisz (eds.), *The Organization of Science and Technology in France, 1808–1914*. Cambridge/Paris: Cambridge University Press/Éditions de la Maison des sciences de l'homme, 1980, pp. 241–82; Stéphane Gerson, *The Pride of Place: Local Memories and Political Culture in Nineteenth-Century France*. Ithaca/London: Cornell University Press, 2003.

5 See Pascale Marie, 'La bibliothèque des Amis de l'instruction du IIIe arrondissement de Paris', in Pierre Nora (ed.), *Les Lieux de mémoire*, vol. I, *La République*. Paris: Gallimard, 1984; Agnès Sanders (ed.), *Des bibliothèques populaires à la lecture publique*. Lyon: Presses de l'Enssib, 2014; and Alan Ritt Baker, 'Les bibliothèques populaires françaises et la connaissance géographique (1860–1900)', in ibid., pp. 283–95.

6 For a detailed study of the Brive working men's library, see Alain Corbin, 'Du capitaine Mayne Reid à Victor Margueritte: l'évolution des lectures populaires en Limousin sous la IIIe République', *Cahier des Annales de Normandie*, 24, in homage to Gabriel Désert, 1992, pp. 453–67.

7 On working men's libraries in the Limousin region, see Alain Corbin, *Archaïsme et modernité en Limousin au XIXe siècle* [1975]. Paris:

Presses universitaires de Limoges, 1998, vol. I, pp. 359–61.

8 Sanders, *Des bibliothèques populaires à la lecture publique*, p. 185.

9 François Chanet, *L'École républicaine et les petites patries*. Paris: Aubier, 1996.

10 Élisée Reclus, 'L'avenir de nos enfants', in Reclus and Pierre Kropotkine, *La Joie d'apprendre*. Geneva: Héros-Limite, 2018, pp. 50, 72, 173–5.

11 See Laurence Guignard, 'Les installations célestes: simulations du cosmos à l'exposition universelle de 1900', in Alexandre Gillet, Estelle Sohier and Jean-François Staszak (eds.), *Simulations du monde: Panoramas, parcs à thème et autres dispositifs immersifs*. Geneva: MétisPresses, 2019, pp. 42–59.

Index

Index

Index

Index

Index

Index

Index

Index